Congratulations
on you!
'21st Birthday'
Mark,
Mum & Dad xxx
All our love,

3 June 2006

The American
AMUSEMENT
PARK

DALE SAMUELSON
WITH WENDY YEGOIANTS

MBI Publishing Company

DEDICATION

To my parents, Joyce and Wendell Samuelson, for introducing me to amusement parks at a very early age, and for believing that my obsession would ultimately be constructive.

ACKNOWLEDGMENTS

Twenty-four years ago, when I first had the idea to write a book, I paid a visit to my cousin Jane Samuelson, who at the time worked for a well-known Chicago publisher. She graciously gave me, from her personal collection, a book about amusement parks that her company had published a few years before. Thanks, Jane!

Any historical undertaking such as this can only be as good as the material available. My deep gratitude goes to those writers who have gone before me, chronicling various aspects of the outdoor amusement business. Without their research on narrow specific topics, a general history of this sort would not be possible. Amusement parks themselves have provided me with great material over the years, and I want to thank to all the hundreds of amusement park owners and personnel who have patiently given me so much of their time over the years.

For their faith and encouragement, I would like to thank Charles Akins, Allen and Liucija Ambrosini, Lee O. Bush, Richard and Carol Munch, and Lena Tabori. For making their collections and photographs available, many thanks go to: Danny Allen; Lee Bush; Frank Czuri; Otto P. Dobnick; Derek Gee and Ralph Lopez of Sharpshooters Productions, authors and publisher of *Laugh Your Troubles Away–The Complete History of Riverview Park*; Tom Halterman; Glenn Lindemer; the Monorail Society; David P. Oroszi; Kim and Carol Pedersen; Mary Lou Rosemeyer of Kennywood Park; Mike Schafer; B. Derek Shaw; Jeffrey Stanton, author of *Venice, California—Coney Island of the Pacific*; and Janice Witherow of Cedar Point. Thanks also to all my fellow postcard dealers for their encouragement, and for helping me find great material over the years.

Most importantly, thank you Andover Junction Publications, the producer of this book. In particular, thanks to the following AJP folks: Steve Esposito for making this all possible; Mike Schafer for his great design and layout; Jim Popson, Paul Magnuson, and Mark Magnuson for technical production matters; and Wendy Yegoiants for her additional research, writing, and proofreading. Thanks also to MBI Publishing Company for the opportunity to write about my favorite subject.—*Dale Samuelson*

First published in 2001 by MBI Publishing Company, Galtier Plaza, Suite 200, 380 Jackson Street, St. Paul, MN 55101-3885 USA.

© Andover Junction Publications, 2001.

Photography by Dale Samuelson except as noted

Editing, design, and layout by Mike Schafer; technical production by Jim Popson; continuity by Wendy Yegoiants, Andover Junction Publications, Blairstown, New Jersey, and Lee, Illinois.

MBI Publishing Company books are also available at discounts in bulk quantity for industrial or sales-promotional use. For details, write to Special Sales Manager at Motorbooks International Wholesalers & Distributors, 729 Prospect Avenue, PO Box 1, Osceola, WI 54020-0001 USA

Library of Congress Cataloging-in-Publication Data available. ISBN: 0-7603-0981-7.

FRONT COVER: Twilight casts a magical aura over Idora Park at Youngstown, Ohio, on a balmy June evening in 1983. Idora was a classic "traditional" amusement park that had been entertaining families, couples, and tourists since the turn of the century. The park's notorious *Wildcat* roller coaster looms like a specter in the evening sky. Through a series of unexpected situations, Idora closed its doors forever in 1984. MIKE SCHAFER. Perched on the bluffs of the Hudson River at Fort Lee, New Jersey, across from New York City, Palisades Park—made famous by the 1962 pop hit "Palisades Park" by Freddy Cannon—was a popular alternative to Coney Island. POSTCARD AND TICKETS, AUTHOR'S COLLECTION

FRONTISPIECE: Without the laughter and shrieking, amusement parks can be lonely places. In the summer of 1984, the *Whip* stands silent among the ruins of abandoned Cascade Park at New Castle, Pennsylvania. MIKE SCHAFER

TITLE PAGE: Considered by many to be America's finest old-fashioned traditional amusement park, Kennywood Park near Pittsburgh, Pennsylvania, glows in the late evening of a summer day in 1980. The last of the crowds are getting their final rides on the *Thunderbolt* roller coaster at left, and then the park will close until the following morning. MIKE SCHAFER

CONTENTS PAGE: The signage that welcomes park-goers comes in many forms: Joyland, Wichita, Kansas (OTTO P. DOBNICK); Lakeside Amusement Park, Denver, Colorado (MIKE SCHAFER); Bell's Amusement Park, Tulsa, Oklahoma (MIKE SCHAFER); Kiddieland, Melrose Park, Illinois (OTTO P. DOBNICK); Euclid Beach, Cleveland, Ohio (LEE O. BUSH COLLECTION); Rockaways' Playland, Rockaway Beach, New York (DALE SAMUELSON). Riders enjoy the *Giant Dipper* coaster at Santa Cruz Beach Boardwalk, Santa Cruz, California, in 1978 (DALE SAMUELSON); Allen Ambrosini and Mike Danshaw take a spin on the *Twister* at Conneaut Lake Park in 1979 (MIKE SCHAFER).

BACK COVER PHOTOS: Park-goers take a plunging ride on the *Tornado* at Adventureland theme park near Des Moines, Iowa, in 1982. MIKE SCHAFER. Dominating Mariner's Landing Pier at Wildwood, New Jersey, is the *Sea Serpent*, a boomerang-type roller coaster. DALE SAMUELSON. Representing a genre of parks that cater exclusively to the under-12 crowd, Kiddieland in west suburban Chicago is one of the best. OTTO P. DOBNICK.

FRONT DUSTJACKET FLAP: Author Dale Samuelson is about to experience the first, terrifying drop of the *Termite*, a home-built roller coaster in the backyard (and on the roof) of the Kim and Carol Pedersen home in Fremont, California. KIM PEDERSEN

END SHEETS: Amusement parks like this at Seal Beach near Los Angeles, California, circa 1925 used to line all three U.S. coasts. In the case of Coney Island at New York City, the brightly lit amusement parks were sometimes the first slice of America that arriving emigrants would see from their ship. AUTHOR'S COLLECTION

Printed in Hong Kong

CONTENTS

FOREWORD...6

INTRODUCTION...7

1
FIRST THINGS FIRST
Pleasure Gardens, Picnic Groves, and Worldly Expos...9

2
CONEY ISLAND
City of Lights, City of Fire...19

3
AN IDEA SPREADS
From Atlantic to Pacific...37

4
HURRY, HURRY
Step Right Up, Folks!...57

5
ROUND AND ROUND
Rides of a Lifetime...77

6
THE KING IS DEAD
Long Live the King!...97

7
GREAT LOST PARKS
May They Rust in Peace...113

8
SURVIVORS
The Traditional Park Lives...127

9
VARIATIONS ON A THEME (PARK)
New Twists on Tradition...145

INDEX...156

FOREWORD

Pontchartrain Beach, New Orleans, Louisiana

Beautiful Pontchartrain Beach amusement park is splashed in late afternoon sun on a summer's day in 1978. The park's venerable Zephyr roller coaster forms a white-timbered backdrop against Pontchartrain's tidy buildings and promenades. Though a popular retreat for the population of New Orleans, the park was sold to developers and torn down to make way for condominiums. They were never built; Pontchartrain Beach could have stayed open. It was a tragedy often repeated with older, traditional parks in America. LEE O. BUSH

Decal from Buckeye Lake, Ohio

Decals and memories are all that remain of this once-popular amusement park near Dayton, Ohio. AUTHOR'S COLLECTION

It is doubtful that the definitive history of amusement parks will ever be written. The subject is so vast and multifaceted as to make a comprehensive work nearly impossible. In one case, the history of one individual park was over twice the size of this volume. Four authors labored for several years to produce it, and when they were done, had so much material left over that they produced a sequel almost as large. And this was for an amusement park that ceased to exist over thirty years ago. Now consider that since the dawn of the amusement park in America over a century ago, there have existed an estimated 3,000-plus amusement parks. In fact, no one knows how many there have been because no one has ever been able to catalog them all. Consider that, at the turn of the twentieth century, small cities all over the country had their own amusement parks, and larger cities often had four or five. Just the task of cataloging them all appears to be a larger job than any one person could complete in a lifetime. Add to that, the individual

history of each park, the vast number of different rides, manufacturers, designers, and showmen, and the fact that amusement park history is still being made each day by the growing numbers of hundreds of existing amusement parks, and we think you get the picture.

In like fashion, this is not to be construed as a comprehensive guide to amusement parks, those that no longer exist, nor those currently operating. Consequently, we want to apologize in advance if we've left out, or not adequately covered, your favorite park. We have endeavored to cover the phenomenon of the American amusement park with an overview of the cultural conditions of their development, a discussion of their makeup, and examples of favorites of the past and present.

The complete history of the amusement park would not only be larger than any Encyclopedia that has ever existed, but would be out of date the instant it was sent to the publisher. So, if it is really such an impossible task, then why even try? We're so glad you asked. This is not the first book on amusement parks, and we doubt that it will be the last. But it is our hope that, by telling this story, we can promote an understanding of the importance of amusement parks to the American way of life. After all, amusement parks are an outgrowth of two other institutions. Fairs and carnivals have always been special events, and as such, have always had a celebratory air about them. It is in this spirit that we approach the American amusement park.

It is our believe that only by understanding their importance to the American family, and the American way of life, can we hope to save them for future generations to enjoy. Amusement parks are all about celebrating life, and there are few things more important than families and friends celebrating together.

—Mike Schafer
Lee, Illinois

INTRODUCTION

People will ask me, "Have you always been interested in amusement parks?" to which I often reply, "Well, not at birth, but shortly after that!" My parents tell me, and I have photos as evidence—one of which is reproduced here—that they took me to a Kiddieland in Manhattan Beach, California, when I was two years old. To them, the look on my face as I rode the rides was one of boredom, resulting in their disappointment that I was not having fun. On the trip home, however, I proceeded to tell them how each and every ride worked, having analyzed all the mechanical machinations. Thus began my lifelong interest in all parks of amusement, as well as my eventual engineering career.

To be sure, my interest in amusement parks has broadened considerably in the passing years. My resulting interest in roller coasters, for example, started out as more architectural than mechanical, and certainly the social and economic issues surrounding the amusement park phenomenon have piqued my historical sensitivities. But these things don't serve to completely explain the seemingly insatiable interest.

More than anything, I think it's the appeal to the senses. The visual design and the sense of motion—the sound of laughter, music, screams of joy/fright, and mechanical whirs, screeches, and bells—the feel of the padded bar in your hands, or your stomach trying to escape through your throat—the smell of French fries and cotton candy—the taste of vanilla swirled with chocolate—these are things we remember. These are the things, in fact, that make those memories unforgettable. This is the magic of the American amusement park.

So what is a "classic" American amusement park? Is it that kiddy park on a vacant lot I visited when I was two, or the dream park in an orange grove that Walt Disney opened the same year? Is it the "beer gardens" of the 1870s, or the Busch Gardens of the 1970s? Luna Park at Coney Island, or Walter Knott's Berry Farm? Riverview or Ocean View? Pacific Ocean Park or Palisades Park? Euclid Beach? Cedar Point? The answer to all these questions is, no—the real answer is, all of them. Although their roots may be in the European pleasure gardens of an earlier time, the classic American amusement park is something else altogether. Like the rides they brought us, their story is a unique one of gasping heights and crashing lows with a few dizzying spins thrown in for good measure. The American amusement park became so successful by the 1920s that we lost count of them, but by the end of the 1960s we could count them all too easily. The 1970s brought new life to amusement parks and started a boom that hasn't seemed to peak yet.

These parks became a reflection of our lives and times. They have appealed to our sense of refinement. They have catered to our darker side. In typical American fashion they have been innovative and prolific—and what they didn't invent, they refined—what they didn't create, they carried to excess. Created for adults and considered for children, the classic American amusement park is perhaps the last vestige of family entertainment.

So take a ride with us, and remember the dizzying heights of the Ferris wheel, the tumultuous tumbles of the roller coaster, and the giddiness of being carried off by prancing steeds on the carousel, for whatever their origins, they are truly American as they were were developed in the American amusement park.

—Dale Samuelson
Santa Ana, California

Author in the making

A very young Dale Samuelson begins a lifelong interest in amusement parks at a Kiddieland in Manhattan Beach, California, in 1955. WENDELL SAMUELSON

Tivoli Gardens, Copenhagen, Denmark

The American amusement park traces its roots to the pleasure gardens of Europe. Beginning as traditional garden settings, they became places that people visited for social interaction as well as relaxation. In time, food services, entertainment, rides and attractions were added. Tivoli is a beautiful example of a centuries-old pleasure park. KIM AND CAROL PEDERSEN

Elitch Gardens, Denver

FACING PAGE: Elitch's modeled its European ancestors by opening as gardens in 1890, and later adding rides. AUTHOR'S COLLECTION

FIRST THINGS FIRST
Pleasure Gardens, Picnic Groves, and Worldly Expos

Tracing the roots of the American amusement park

The quest for amusement is undoubtedly as old as humankind itself, and almost every form of entertainment that has been tried appears in some form, with varying success, in the amusement park. Activities as diverse as concerts, bowling, stage shows, horse and auto racing, gambling, sharpshooting, picnicking, movie watching, drinking, dancing, dining, roller skating, boating, flying, and myriad other participatory sports have all been major draws for amusement parks throughout their history. To trace the roots of the American amusement park, we'll turn back the clock to the 1500s.

Toboggan Slide—Château Frontenac et Glissoire, Québec, Canada.--47.

Toboggan Slide, Canada

The Russian ice slide of the seventeenth century is considered to be the ancestor of the modern roller coaster. Shown here is an early twentieth century view of the same ride, referred to as a Toboggan Slide. Coincidently, many early figure-8 roller coasters were called toboggan rides. In fact, the Philadelphia Toboggan Company, founded in 1904 to build toboggan coasters, still exists today as PTC, building modern roller coaster cars. AUTHOR'S COLLECTION

Pleasure wheel, Egypt

This primitive pleasure wheel was located in Egypt around the turn of the twentieth century. While it dates from an era after the introduction of the World's Columbian Exposition Ferris wheel in 1893, it is a sterling example of a hand-powered wooden wonder, essentially unchanged for four centuries. AUTHOR'S COLLECTION

European Pleasure Gardens

The roots of the modern inception of the American amusement park began in sixteenth century Europe. Traditional public spaces trimmed with flowers and trees became pleasure gardens in France when sporting activities were added. Refreshment stands followed next and illumination for extended evening use first appeared here. In England, taverns and inns grew into pleasure gardens at the time of the British Industrial Revolution during the late eighteenth century. As they developed, their hallmarks became intricate landscaping, fanciful structures, extensive illumination, theatrical presentations, concerts, balloon ascensions, and fireworks displays.

In 1661 New Spring Garden was the first of these new parks to achieve international acclaim in London. It was renovated and renamed Vauxhall Gardens in 1728, and in the 1730s the first entry fee—one shilling—was established. Garden walks, arbors, mazes, shops, dining pavilions, paintings, statuary and replicas of ruins not only entertained patrons, but set the tone for future centuries of amusement park attractions. Music, dancing, sports and spectacles were the amusements of the times, in a place where aristocrats freely and willingly mingled with the merchant and working classes. Critics claimed that Vauxhall and its counterparts were becoming centers of vice and social infection, but it was the thrill of unpredictable encounters and the socio-political intercourse available that drew many, and set the stage for future development in public entertainment. The Gardens lasted nearly two centuries, and made a grandiose exit in 1859, closing with a fireworks display that read FAREWELL FOREVER.

As the park concept took shape, the foundation for future thrill rides was also formulating. Coasting devices in the form of constructed ice slides are known to have existed in seventeenth century Russia and are believed to have existed as early as the fifteenth century. By the early 1800s, coasting structures—known as Russian Mountains—were appearing all over Europe. In a small town in what is now Bulgaria, a primitive precursor to the Ferris Wheel was discovered and sketched by a traveling Englishman, in use in 1620! And the earliest known carousel-type ride dates back to 500 A.D.!

Denmark was also a forerunning influence on the world's amusement parks. Bakken, one of the first European parks, still exists near Copenhagen and claims to have opened in 1583, making it the oldest operating amusement park in the world. World famous Tivoli Gardens, another Copenhagen landmark, has most certainly affected the amusement park scene. Aside from being a beautiful example of a traditional European park, still operating many classic old rides, it is said to have been a strong influence on Walt Disney. After visiting Tivoli in 1950, Disney's vision for his Mickey Mouse Park (the original name, believe it or not!) changed dramatically. As Tivoli reflects an earlier Eurasia, Disneyland would soon reflect, if not magnify, the roots (and branches) of American history.

Two influences—one broad, the other specific—effected the development of the amusement park in America more than any others. The Industrial Revolution supplied the means, and the World's Fairs provided the model.

Industrial Evolution

Many historians believe that the Industrial Revolution of the late 1700s is a misnomer, insisting it was instead part of industrial *evolution*. In any case, major railroad development in the early and mid 1800s lead to a second industrial revolution later in that century. The resulting availability of electricity, the improvement of mechanical prowess, changing work patterns and demographics, and the resulting increase in leisure time were the catalysts for a new, more complex form of amusement.

The Industrial Revolution also caused a cultural revolution. By the turn of the century, the country was experiencing a dramatic shift from an agrarian society to an urban-industrial culture. Specifically, industrialization prompted the spectacular and rapid growth of a working population that would ultimately become the middle-class backbone of the country. The major effects of this shift were increased spending money and spare time amongst a class of people who previously had neither. A consequential cultural revolt against the reigning genteel standards of taste and conduct was in full swing by the 1920s.

The genteel self-conscious elite that had assumed cultural leadership throughout most of the nineteenth century, did not give up that position easily. Ruling—at least in their minds—as the official culture, they believed that all activities, both work and leisure, should ultimately be constructive. These reformers, as they became known,

took it upon themselves to instruct, refine and discipline this new urban-industrial society by preaching the Victorian values of moral integrity, self-control, and industriousness to the masses.

The architects of public amusement that were at work in the late 1800s, embraced this reformist vision. They sought not simply to amuse, but to instruct the populous in lessons of aesthetic taste and social responsibility. In an effort to inspire in what they deemed a fractious people, a respect for cultural standards, they presented a model of social order, cohesion and tranquility. In essence,

Tivoli Gardens theming
It has been said that when Walt Disney visited Tivoli in 1950, his concept for what would become Disneyland changed dramatically. The structure of Disneyland jelled quickly, once Walt settled on the idea of stylized and themed "lands," paying special attention to architecture and landscaping. Disney would use typical American themes in a way similar to Tivoli's use of Eurasian themes in the design of its attractions. KIM AND CAROL PEDERSEN

they believed that simply by manipulating an environment, they could elevate public taste and reform public conduct. Chief among these architects was Frederick Law Olmsted.

As architect of New York City's Central Park, the first major public park in the United States, Olmsted attempted to counteract the effects of urban mass society. He had observed on the street that people passed each other without any interaction. This was the impetus for his concept of democratic recreation which is embodied in the design of Central Park. From Olmsted's perspective, the park would serve as an easily accessible rural refuge from the day-to-day city pressures. Primary recreational value was to stem from the contemplation of natural scenery—-picturesque woods, rolling hills, pastoral meadows and lakes—viewed from meandering paths. He made no provision for the working-class need and desire for more manly physical sports. What Olmsted failed to see, or at least chose initially to ignore, was that Americans had been working hard for four hundred years: now they wanted to play. He would soon come inadvertently to that realization.

World's Fairs

Since their inception, world's fairs have by definition been showcases of technology and ingenuity. The 1876 Centennial Exposition in Philadelphia featured exciting new developments in amusements. Looking like a steam train partially split down the center, an early monorail rode on a single beam supported by a wooden trestle. Although it was designed to spotlight a new transportation system, it more accurately

Early park monorail
Looking somewhat like a steam locomotive straddling a trestle, this early monorail actually ran at Philadelphia's 1876 Centennial Exposition. It would be 81 years before a monorail ride would appear at an amusement or entertainment-type park, at Summit Beach Park in Akron, Ohio. Two years later, Walt Disney would make it a staple theme-park ride. COURTESY THE MONORAIL SOCIETY

foreshadowed a popular and successful contemporary amusement ride: the elevated monorail that carries passengers on a treetop sightseeing trip around the park (or in the case of Walt Disney World, between the park and hotels). The Exposition also spawned the Sawyer Observatory, where steam-powered elevators lifted fairgoers to the top of the 300-foot tower. After the fair closed, the Sawyer Observatory was moved to Coney Island, New York, and renamed the Iron Tower.

The most significant changes in the development and presentation of amusements came from Chicago and its 1893 World's Columbian Exposition. The Columbian Exposition was organized as a celebration of four centuries of development in the New World, but in reality expressed the vision of the social and cultural elite that seemed eager to recreate society in its own image. Daniel H. Burnham, from the establishment that became known as the Chicago School of Architecture, and Frederick Olmsted—by this time America's most eminent landscape architect—led the fair planners with a sense that they were embarking upon an aesthetic collaboration that would transform society. In the exposition they saw an opportunity to construct an ideal that would purify the gross materialism of American culture, order its chaotic energies, and uplift its character and taste. The majority of the exposition's architects, sculptors, and artists had received their formal training at the Ecole des Beaux-Arts in Paris, where they had absorbed a respect for tradition, proportion, symmetry, and grandeur. In their minds their art represented not only a visual preference, but a cultural ideal.

But the planners had a problem. The 1889 Exposition in Paris, France, had produced the Eiffel Tower, a magnificent engineering triumph, and the Columbian Exposition's board of directors were looking for something spectacular to equal, if not surpass, the Parisians. Though pleasure wheels had existed for centuries, and in fact at least one other engineer had already proposed an enormous pleasure wheel to the board, George Washington Gale Ferris Jr. envisioned a ride so outrageous as to literally change the name of pleasure wheels forever. While it is the only wheel Ferris ever designed, at 250 feet in diameter with 36 gondolas holding 60 passengers each—a total capacity of 2,160 passengers—it made such an impression that pleasure wheels are forever referred to as Ferris wheels, regardless of their stature.

To be sure, the "big wheel" idea was controversial among the fair-planners. Rides have been a part of regional fairs since their inception, but the primitive nature of the rides at these agricultural fairs was not the kind of thing that these urbanite fair-planners wished to have associated with their worldly exposition. The planners would have been content with their aesthetically spectacular "White City" area of the exposition—a huge central lagoon surrounded by marvelous pavilions done in the new Beaux Arts style—housing states' and countries' exhibits. However, with the advent of rides like the Scenic Railways of the 1880s, mechanical amusements were becoming a more significant draw to patrons of amusement places. It had long been believed that to educate the masses, they must first be entertained. If this world's fair was to draw beyond the upper crust, the great wheel would have to be built.

At the great Chicago Exposition, other amusements were organized around Ferris's wheel. This new concept, called the Midway Plaisance—a large array of rides, attractions, and concessions—was a big success. It was such a success, that it was

seen by so many people, that virtually all subsequent American amusement parks would henceforth adopt the concept of the midway in organizing attractions. It is unknown how many purveyors of amusements attended the fair that year, but two known attendees—George Tilyou and Captain Paul Boyton—blazed pioneer trails in the amusement park business.

Tilyou's family had been involved at Coney Island, New York, since the early days of the beach bathhouses. Upon reportedly attempting and failing to purchase the Ferris wheel from the Columbian Exposition, George Tilyou returned to Coney Island and erected a sign that stated: "On This Site Will Be Erected The World's Largest Ferris Wheel." He would go on to develop Steeplechase Park, one of the most unique and successful amusement parks ever built. And in 1895, Boyton would borrow the concept of the midway and open what is believed to be the beginning of the modern amusement park. These two men, utilizing the Midway structural organization of attractions at two different parks, would forever change the amusement park industry.

1893 World's Columbian Exposition, Chicago

The 1893 World's Fair at Chicago had a profound effect on American architecture and amusement parks, among other things. The exhibition grounds were located at what is today Jackson Park at 55th Street—today's Museum of Science and Industry site. (The museum is a replica of one of the exhibition buildings.) In this watercolor done expressly for sale at the exhibition by artist C. Graham, we see the grounds as viewed eastward from atop the Ferris wheel. Lake Michigan is in the distance. In the foreground is the Midway Plaisance, which is still in place, minus the buildings and concessions. NINA SWANSON

Two anecdotes of the Chicago fair would color the future of amusement parks. First, from the elite perspective, the concept and execution of the White City was a triumph of uniformity over diversity and inventiveness. But diversity and inventiveness are what has made America great, and in fact, much of the architectural community of that era viewed the White City as aristocratic and alien to the American experience. The grandeur of White City's Court of Honor suggested stature, power and permanence. However, even before the end of the fair's five-month run, most of the White City's 400 structures, having been built of staff (plaster and latticework), were showing signs of decay. Further, as Olmsted toured the White City, he discovered on fairgoers' faces the same tired, dutiful looks that he had seen on the streets of New York—the visage he had tried to counteract with his park design. Ultimately, Olmsted urged Burnham to introduce festive elements from, of all places, the Midway, to the White City. The fair's planners were forced to admit that private commercial attractions were more popular than the White City's free cultural exhibits. People came to the fair to have fun.

The other interesting sidebar is a rather obscure theme-park reference. It seems that Elias Disney moved his family from the Kissimmee, Florida, area—the future home of Walt Disney World—to Chicago, to obtain work as a carpenter during the construction of the exposition. Elias was so thankful for the work opportunity, that when Walt's brother Roy was born during the fair, Elias wanted to name him Columbus. It can only be presumed that Elias' wife Flora, talked him out of it. Walt was also born in Chicago, but not until 1901, and shortly thereafter moved with the family to Marceline, Missouri. There is, of course, no direct connection between the Columbian Exposition and Disneyland, but one can't help but wonder what the effect on Walt's life would have been had his family stayed in Florida.

As for the Beaux Arts style of architecture introduced to America through the Columbian Exposition, it caught on in a big way in day-to-day America, particularly in the construction of public buildings, such as New York's famous Grand Central Terminal. However, its application in amusement centers that followed the Columbian Exposition was minimal.

They've been working on the railroad

Railroads were critical to America's growth in the 1800s and most of the twentieth century, and thus were key to the development of early amusement parks. In fact, what is often cited as the first American roller coaster was America's second railroad, appearing in 1826 (Chapter 6), well before the amusement park idea caught on. Until

World War I, 98 percent of all intercity travel in the U.S. was by rail, so most travel to resorts and amusement areas was done via the trains or cars of a steam railway or "traction" (electric interurban or trolley) company. (Frank Sprague's development of the traction motor in the 1880s made electric-powered trolleys successful, hence the "traction" name.)

Some historians credit traction companies or the utility companies that usually owned them with the development of the amusement park as an American institution. With our modern systems of protection from (non-government-sponsored) monopolies, it can be hard to imagine how things worked over a century ago. Utility companies then were powerful entities that often owned or otherwise controlled non-utility businesses, notably city streetcar companies or interurban (city-to-city) railways, both of which were almost universally electric-powered.

Utility companies often charged their subsidiary traction or interurban companies a flat rate for electric power, which could be a bane or blessing depending on the viewpoint of traction-company management. Ordinarily, trolley and interurban ridership was highest on weekdays and most of the trolley cars and interurban trains sat dormant on weekends. Since electric power was the single highest operating expense, any increase in weekend fares would be almost pure profit. But how could traction companies entice the public to ride their trolleys on Saturdays and Sundays? By building a leisure-time attraction at an outlying location along the line. Numerous amusement parks got their start this way, with traction companies buying the land and then designing, building, and operating picnic or amusement parks. The picnic parks themselves often evolved into amusement complexes.

THE BEACH, LAKE TAKADIP, RIVERSIDE PARK, SPRINGFIELD, MASS.

Riverside Park, Agawam (Springfield), Massachusetts

Opened circa 1840 and later for a time operated as a trolley park, Riverside should be a candidate for status as America's oldest amusement park. Unfortunately it closed during the Great Depression. It was purchased and reopened in 1940 and operated as Riverside for nearly six decades before being turned into Six Flags New England by its new owners, Premier Parks. AUTHOR'S COLLECTION

Whalom Park, Lunenburg (Fitchburg), Massachusetts

Opened in 1893, Whalom Park is to this day one of the finest examples of the small local amusement park. While the toboggan slide shown is gone, Whalom continues to be a repository for some of the most historic rides in existence. AUTHOR'S COLLECTION

PONCE DE LEON PARK, ATLANTA, GA.

Ponce de Leon Park, Atlanta, Georgia

Many early amusement parks started out as picnic groves. As the groves became popular meeting places, the growing customer base obliged park owners to add other attractions. In this early twentieth century view of Ponce de Leon, we see the picnic pavilions that allowed large groups of people to dine together. Most traditional amusement parks have not only allowed patrons to bring food in from outside, but have encouraged it. Many of the remaining smaller traditional parks still rely on picnics for a large percentage of their business. Even some of the larger traditional parks like Lagoon in Farmington, Utah, and Kennywood Park outside Pittsburgh, still have huge picnic pavilions like those shown here. Bringing your own food remains an experience unique to traditional parks, however, as most theme parks don't allow it. AUTHOR'S COLLECTION

American Picnic Groves

Just where did the American amusement park get its start? Exactly where the idea came from—and who had it first—will probably never be known for certain, but there are some specific landmarks that reveal developing trends.

The common thread among the beginnings of most amusement parks, is that they started out not initially as ride parks, but as resorts. Resorts like Newport, Rhode Island, existed before the Revolutionary War, but around 1830, railroads, canals, and steamboats gradually made a broader range of resorts more accessible. Long Branch, New Jersey, Nahant, Massachusetts, and Saratoga Springs, New York, were among the resorts of the time, but they catered to a moneyed crowd who could afford the expensive accommodations and the travel and time to get there. In general, it was not entertainment but the opportunities for social encounter that made these resorts popular with the upper-class visitors. Although not all of these resorts eventually turned directly into amusement parks, the elite did establish certain locations as destinations that would later be overrun by the masses.

As the century moved on, resorts that catered to a burgeoning middle class began to evolve. Woods, beaches, and park-like gardens were the first attractions; food and drink vendors usually followed. Most of the resorts that developed in the mid-1800s were on the outskirts of cities, making them a convenient day-trip getaway from the noise and crowds of daily reality. Before long, many of them were building hotels to entice patrons to stay longer. Most of the early activities were adult-oriented, beer drinking and gaming chief among them. Soon, animal rides and playground equipment like swings and crude merry-go-rounds geared toward children were sprouting up in various locations, and the seed of the modern amusement park began to germinate.

The pleasure gardens of Europe had a direct influence on the development of the American amusement park. Vauxhall Gardens—built in the 1850s in the area that became New York's Bowery—took its name from a then famous Vauxhall

Gardens in Paris, the Parisians having "borrowed" the name from the original Londoners'. The New Jersey and New York bathing resorts—including Coney Island—were started in the 1850s and 1860s, and developed into full-scale amusement centers by the early 1900s.

In one of our examples, transition from garden to amusement park began, appropriately, in an apple orchard. James Parker was the owner of an orchard on the Ohio River. He found opening Parker's Island to picnickers was more profitable than just harvesting apples. He later added a dance hall, bowling alley, and shooting gallery, and by the mid 1880s, it had become known as Ohio Grove, the "Coney Island of the West." The Ohio Grove moniker didn't stick however, and it eventually became known as Cincinnati's Coney Island until it was dismantled after the 1970 season.

It's not surprising that the early amusement parks were developed in the most densely populated area of the country, and New England lays claim to two of the first. On the Connecticut River, near Springfield, Massachusetts, a picnic ground and recreation area called Gallup's Grove opened in 1840. By the early 1900s, it was known as Riverside Grove and featured boat rides on the river, a large swimming pool called Lake Takadip, and a ballroom with a capacity of 4,500 dancers. By 1928, Riverside Park, as it was then called, also featured as many as four roller coasters. By 1933 however, the Great Depression had taken its toll and the park closed. In 1940, one hundred years after the original opening, the property was purchased and reopened as Riverside Park. It operated for 60 seasons and is now known as Six Flags New England.

Another early New England park, which started six years after Riverside's original opening, still flourishes. In 1684, the Norton family acquired property in Bristol, Connecticut, from Chief Compound, leader of the Tunxis Indians. For generations the family used the lake for personal summer recreation, and, in 1846, Gad Norton organized Lake Compounce as a commercial bathing beach and concert grove. Having survived a troubling century and a half, including uncertain changes in ownership in the 1980s and 1990s, it today holds the prestigious position as America's oldest continuously operated amusement park.

The place commonly accepted as the first large-scale amusement resort was Jones Wood, located along the East River in Manhattan. Begun in the early 1800s and covering over 150 acres, it was a prime example of the American amusement park in microcosm. The most popular amusement at these early resorts was beer drinking, and it was at Jones Wood that the term "beer garden"—an offshoot of the pleasure garden—is believed to have been coined. Although children's rides were offered, the combination of beer and participatory sports like shooting galleries and wrestling matches caused it to become a rather rowdy place. Instead, most families chose to escape the heat and oppression of the city by heading for the seaside resorts that were springing up along the coast. As so many parks built on the outskirts of cities would later come to face themselves, rapid development and the resulting high land prices pressed Jones Wood out of business, and in the 1860s it just sort of vanished.

At the same time, however, just across town on the southwestern end of Long Island, a new resort was forming. The small island of sand dunes where Henry Hudson landed his ships in 1609 was becoming the most famous amusement area the world has ever known.

Columbia Gardens, Butte, Montana

Beginning with a traditional garden setting, Columbia Gardens added a few rides to create a beautiful amusement park. As long as it lasted, Columbia Gardens never lost sight of the fact that its natural beauty was its biggest asset. AUTHOR'S COLLECTION

Luna Park, Coney Island, New York

Coney Island itself was not an amusement park, but an amusement area comprised of several different parks and independent attractions. This rendering depicts one of Coney's most famous establishments—Luna Park—around the turn of the century. Its international flair and sometimes whimsical design would inspire numerous imitations. AUTHOR'S COLLECTION

Coney Island Cyclone

FACING PAGE: A Coney Island classic since 1927, the Cyclone roller coaster today defines Coney Island. MIKE SCHAFER

CONEY ISLAND
City of Lights, City of Fire

How a beach in Brooklyn, New York, set the tone for the American amusement park

Coney Island was not the World's nor America's first amusement park. In fact, Coney Island, in its entire history, never has been an amusement park. It's not even an island anymore. What Coney Island is, and always has been, is a collection of amusements. First came a hotel, then bathhouses, then more hotels and restaurants, casinos, racetracks, rides and attractions— and finally, several distinctly separate walled and gated amusement parks.

It's easy to understand the misconceptions about Coney Island. It has been, through the years, so many

Bathing Beach, Coney Island, N. Y.

Coney Island's bathing beach
As this 1920s postcard view shows, Coney Island would be a popular place even without the amusements. In fact, the beach itself was Coney's first attraction. Coney is oriented with a southern exposure so that the sun shines on its beach from morning to dusk. With the arrival of the subway/elevated to Coney Island in 1920, New Yorkers could reach the beach in a short time for only a nickel. During the 1920s and 1930s, it was not unusual to see a million people at Coney on a summer Sunday. AUTHOR'S COLLECTION

things to so many people. It stands on the edge of what is not only the largest city in America, but also its cultural capital. How could Coney Island be anything less than spectacular? After all, it is the birthplace of the modern roller coaster, the gated amusement park, and the hot dog!

Coney Island was created as a playground for New Yorkers, if not the world that came to visit. Five miles of beach spread out latitudinally so that all summer long, from dawn to dusk, the entire length of the strand was washed in full sun. As a sheltered basin, Coney's beach had been piled with sand, making it an ideal spot for bathing adjacent to America's most populous city.

In the years prior to the Civil War, Coney Island was a lonely place. Yet by the time the war had commenced, a small steamship was carrying passengers to its west end. Before the war was over, Coney Island Point had become a hangout for New York City's counctercultures. Here gamblers, confidence men, pickpockets, roughnecks, and prostitutes plied their trades outside the reach of city officials.

In the decades after the Civil War, investors discovered the potential of Coney Island as a resort, and money started flowing in. The number of steamboat and railroad lines increased, and large opulent hotels began to spring up along the shoreline. To create a more enticing reputation, the developments assumed new names. Coney Island Point became Nortons Point, and then the

West End. West Brighton, Brighton Beach, and Manhattan Beach followed eastward. In time, the West End faded in prominence, and Brighton and Manhattan beaches took on greater levels of respectability. Sporting their own private railroads, Manhattan and Brighton Beaches were, for the most part, successful in seceding from the taint and ill-reputed reputation of Coney Island. West Brighton was the site of the first hotel—the Coney Island House—and what would eventually become the Coney New Yorkers would know and love. The name Coney Island stuck and West Brighton faded into history.

It is hard to overstate the significance of Coney Island's contribution to the shaping of modern culture. During its heyday, urban America came of age as an industrial society and people began to adjust to a new lifestyle. That era began in earnest in 1895 with what would later be transformed into the first of Coney's famous amusement parks—Sea Lion Park. Although Coney Island was not the first place to develop the roots of the modern amusement park, it was the source from which many new ideas sprang. Coney developed the models and then proceeded to reflect and reshape the ensuing cultural changes, only to once again reshape and reflect further.

The second Industrial Revolution was generating a social shift from production to consumption, and greater opportunities for play. But Americans hadn't really learned how to play. In the days before automobiles, families would plan for weeks before embarking on a one-day trip, and then having arrived at their destination, were generally at a loss as to how to amuse themselves. Coney took on the role of instructor, giving first New Yorkers and then the rest of the country lessons in fun.

What's in a name?

The name Coney Island is an enigma. Two theories exist about the origin of the famous moniker. Some believe that the island was named after an early Dutch settler named Coneynen. Others say it was the huge numbers of wild rabbits or conies (*Konijn* in Dutch) that inhabited the area that lent the island its name. Either way, today it is an island in name only. Coney *was* an island at one time, separated from the rest of Brooklyn by Coney Island Creek, but between the ravaging of storms and man, the creek has long since been obliterated, though the name remains.

The name Coney Island, as well as the names of its three major parks—Luna, Steeplechase, and

Dreamland—have been borrowed or stolen and used for other parks all over the world. To this day, Coney Island Hot Dogs, Coney Island Taffy, and Coney Island Custard are found everywhere. Such has been the impact of what had been an insignificant small strip of land that in the early 1800s was frequented only by rabbit hunters!

Although the name has always been popular, Coney Island itself has been known by many other labels. The most popular references through the years have been Sodom by the Sea, City of Fire, and the Nickel Empire. In many ways, the incredible history of Coney Island is encapsulated in the stories behind these titles.

Sodom By the Sea: the early years

Coney Island's first inhabitants were undoubtedly the rabbits, and sometime thereafter, their hunters. In 1829 the Coney Island House came to be perched upon the lonely dunes of Coney. Its fame spread among the elite. Washington Irving, Herman Melville, Edgar Allen Poe, John C. Calhoun, Henry Clay, Daniel Webster, Sam Houston, P. T. Barnum, and Walt Whitman were among the early visitors to enjoy the unmatched and unobstructed view of the harbor. But in general, New Yorkers were so busy they hadn't even noticed Coney. James Gordon Bennett, publisher of the *New York Herald*, was among these early visitors, but held a differing view. Upon sniffing the air, Bennett wrinkled his nose and declared the Island objectionable, sandy, clammy, and fishy. One man's objection, however, is another man's objective, and the sand, clams, and fish soon became among the very things that New Yorkers clamored for. A second hotel and a restaurant on the beach soon followed.

In 1867, a young man named John Y. McKane was elected as a town constable for the community of Gravesend, a small farming community south of Brooklyn, jurisdiction of which Coney Island fell into. To Gravesenders, Coney Island was merely a piece of sand to the south, not suitable for farming. The town commissioners, in fact, had been leasing Coney Island oceanfront lots for as little as three dollars a year. John McKane, who was destined to become, as one writer put it—Grand Pooh-Bah of Coney Island—thought they were undervalued.

A carpenter by trade, McKane had started his own construction business just a year before his election as constable. As development of Coney progressed, McKane kept busy slapping together rustic bathing pavilions and the ramshackle shelter beer saloons that began crowding the beach. His attention to the undervalued rental of the common land of Coney Island got him elected, in 1869, as one of the three town commissioners. By the next Gravesend annual meeting, he was able to report that the rental income for the common lands had increased 100 percent. By the following year, McKane's report had become the highlight of the town's annual meetings. The Gravesenders looked at their new commissioner with the utmost respect.

The rush to the beach had officially begun. At first it came to Coney Island Point, at the western tip of the island, primarily because this was the location of the first steamboat pier. On the point, the restaurant was cool and clean, clams (and chowder) were plentiful and tasty, the beach was superb, and rental bathing suits were available for 25 cents.

All too soon, though, the rowdies of New York City—the gamblers, pickpockets, strong-arm and confidence men—had discovered the joys of the waves and sun, and the prostitutes found a pleasant and prosperous place to ply their trade. Whatever righteous indignation arose only

Surf Avenue, Coney Island

The railroad first arrived at Coney Island in 1875. By the following year there were six separate rail lines to Coney, either running or near completion. These evolved into, or were replaced by streetcar lines, and by 1920, the subway had arrived. This early 1920s view down Surf Avenue shows just three popular methods of transport to Coney Island—trolleys, buses, and autos. It also shows how crowded the amusements had become. AUTHOR'S COLLECTION

served to pique the interest of the curious. Every weekend thousands flocked to see what the ruckus was all about.

As commissioner of the common lands, McKane took a *laissez-faire* attitude toward the whole thing. As far as McKane was concerned, what he didn't see, didn't hurt anybody, and those who didn't like what went on there could just stay away. But the big gamblers, New York politicians, and their guests continued to come in droves—and in 1873 Coney Island Point, which had rented for $400 a year, now went for $6,100 in a lease that McKane made with a close friend of Brooklyn's democratic boss.

The biggest boost to Coney Island's early popularity was the arrival of the railroad in 1875. By consolidating a number of smaller lines, Andrew Culver created the Prospect Park & Coney Island Railroad and in his first year brought one million visitors to Coney. After bringing two million the second year, and fearful that the ocean would not be enough to amuse the throngs, Culver brought the Sawyer Observatory from the Centennial Exposition in Philadelphia. Renamed the 300-foot Iron Tower, with two steam-powered elevators and a telescopic eye on top, it is considered the first mechanical amusement on Coney Island. By 1876, not only was the recently completed Ocean Parkway conveying anyone with carriage and conviction from Brooklyn's Prospect Park straight to the island, but no less than six separate railways were either bringing patrons or about to.

By 1876 the Gravesend elders were on to McKane. But between the Coney Island lessees and McKane's own staff, he still had enough support at election time to put him in the office of Supervisor. The Supervisor was, by default, chairman of the Town Board, the Board of Health, the Water Board, the Improvement Board, and the Board of Audit. The nation's grandest playground was now McKane's toy.

Once the "Tweed Ring" of politicians was ousted from New York in the mid 1870s, professional thieves of all sorts, including known bank robbers, headed for Coney. McKane had handed them licenses to operate saloons, hotels, and gambling joints. Some even joined the police force. Amid this environment Coney Island earned its reputation as the roughest place on earth. Its nightly goings on not only caused overcrowding, but gave rise to the title of Sodom by the Sea.

Pomposity and hyperbole ruled the day at Coney Island. The West Brighton Hotel advertised a kitchen capable of serving 8,000 people daily. The Sea Beach Palace boasted it could serve 15,000 dinners at a sitting and accommodate 10,000 overnight guests. The Ocean Pavilion, owned by Charles Feltman of hot dog fame, billed itself as the largest building on Coney Island: home to a ballroom for 3,000 dancers, a piazza for 5,000 onlookers, a dining room for 8,000, and rooms for 20,000 guests. Incredible!

The beginning of the end for McKane was November 7, 1893, election day. McKane had managed to register over 6,000 voters in his Gravesend district. Considering that the town's population was only about 8,400, it is likely that only 1,500 were legitimate. In fact, the *New York Times* had publicly questioned his numbers. Before dawn on election day, McKane was forming his welcoming party for the republican poll watchers he had been warned were to show up. When, just before dawn, three carriages arrived with the intruders, McKane had 300 troops, 50 of them in police uniform, blocking town hall.

The buggies pulled up, and out stepped Colonel Alexander Bacon, the chairman of a legislative committee that had exposed McKane five years prior. When Bacon presented an injunction, McKane responded with "Injunctions don't go here." Bacon and his party were subsequently beaten. The next day, McKane's dictum was a feature headline in Brooklyn. Before the day was over, the wire services had picked it up and the whole country knew about it. Despite McKane's

efforts at the polls, reformers were swept into office at all levels. Before the end of the year, a grand jury handed up indictments of eleven counts against McKane. Two months later, McKane was on his way to Sing Sing.

Undoubtedly, McKane was guilty of many crimes. Unquestionably the most egregious was the theft of Coney Island's good name. The lovely beach had been tainted irrevocably. Though having passed many lips already, it was the *New York Times* that indelibly offered the nickname Sodom by the Sea. After McKane's departure, figurative brimstone in the form of literal fire ravaged the entertainment area of West Brighton in 1893, and again in 1895. Purified of both its political corruption, and most of the lawless entertainment, Sodom by the Sea lay, if not truly dead, at least mortally wounded. Coney Island was now poised on the edge of a new era. The coming decade

was to see the creation of the three most amazing amusement parks that the Americas have ever known.

A price tag on fun

Historically, parks have been split over admission policies. Picnic parks—whose primary income was from the use of the park grounds itself—generally charged a nominal admission, while ride parks—which were often open parks—charged only for rides and attractions. Some parks—like Conneaut Lake Park in western Pennsylvania and Dorney Park in Allentown, Pennsylvania—had public roads running through the middle of them and only in recent years have gated the parks to charge admission. Other parks—notably Knoebels Amusement Resort in central Pennsylvania, the seaside parks in California, and the amusement piers of the New Jersey coast—remain open-access parks to this day.

Sometimes history turns full circle. In the late 1960s the Knott family had a problem at their Berry-Farm-turned-Ghost-Town-theme-park. The open gate created a haven for a large number of transients (calling themselves hippies). In 1968 it seemed the only practical way to alleviate the problem was to fence-in the park and charge

Shoot-the-Chutes

This was the centerpiece ride that Captain Paul Boyton developed for his Sea Lion Park. Thompson and Dundy thought it was the only thing worth salvaging when they took over after the 1902 season. In 1903, when they opened Luna Park, it was again the centerpiece. It was to become the centerpiece ride for parks all over the world. Passengers rode to the top on the funicular railway to the right. AUTHOR'S COLLECTION

Loop the Loop

Going upside down (on purpose) was introduced to America in 1895 with Lina Beecher's Flip Flap coaster at Sea Lion Park. The 25-foot true-circle loop made for an uncomfortable ride, and the four-rider capacity made for an unprofitable one. In 1901, on West Tenth Avenue, Edward Prescott introduced the Loop the Loop. With an elliptical loop and a four-rider capacity, it was a more comfortable ride, but still not profitable. AUTHOR'S COLLECTION

Steeplechase, the funny face

The grinning face (some would say it was done in George Tilyou's likeness) emblem became an icon of Steeplechase Park. Although the park had been gone for years, this newly completed Steeplechase mural on a building wall at Coney Island in 1985 reincarnated the imagery of the once-famous amusement center. OTTO P. DOBNICK

Entrance to Steeplechase, 1905

Countless fun-seekers walked beneath the toothy-grinned face at the entrance of Steeplechase Park during its 67-year history. To little kids, it was probably a pretty scary-looking countenance, but once inside the elaborate park, their troubles were forgotten. AUTHOR'S COLLECTION

admission. Some 70 years earlier, George Tilyou observed a similar situation at Coney Island. He watched with curiosity as Captain Paul Boyton attempted to resolve this issue at his new park.

Sea Lion Park

A spinoff of Captain Paul Boyton's internationally acclaimed traveling aquatic circus, Sea Lion Park was opened on July 4, 1895. It is considered the first gated amusement park in America (and probably the world) where an admission was charged at the gate. The park's name came from the feature attraction: Boyton's 40 trained juggling and racing sea lions (a harbinger of the marine parks and aquariums that are popular today). He was well known for his previous achievements as a daring navigator and the world's original frogman, swimming across the English Channel and other major bodies of water in an inflated rubber suit. Boyton brought his ingenuity to Sea Lion Park by introducing a ride called the *Shoot-the-Chutes*, which would be replicated throughout the world.

This water ride consisted of flat-bottomed boats that careened down a steep, wild slide splashing a dozen riders on their way to a lagoon below, where they then hit a slight upcurve and were bounced and soaked to the amusement of the less brave spectators.

The 16-acre Sea Lion Park also contributed to amusement park history with its scariest offering: the *Flip-Flap*. A new twist in roller coasters, the *Flip-Flap* was a centrifugal pleasure railway invention of Lina Beecher. A four-passenger car raced down an incline and completed a 25-foot diameter loop before cruising back into the station. The ride attracted a great deal of attention, but before it was improved upon numerous patrons complained of the mild whiplash that came as an unfortunate side effect of the head-over-heels thrill.

The *Loop the Loop*, invented by Edward Prescott, was the *Flip-Flap*'s logical and somewhat safer offspring, and became a major attraction for riders and not so courageous spectators alike when it began operation on West Tenth Avenue in 1901. A more effective use of centrifugal force, the core of the *Loop the Loop* was an ellipse rather than a circle.

Advertisement bills claimed it was "the safest and the greatest sensation of the age" and guaranteed "no danger whatever," but the public was not convinced. And because the *Loop the Loop*'s capacity was small, taking on only four brave

souls per circuit, it could not generate revenue at a fast enough rate to work off the debt incurred to erect the attraction.

Boyton added an old mill ride, the *Cages of Wild Wolves*, and in 1899, a grand ballroom. The additions stepped up Sea Lion Park's popularity, but it was still only a modest financial success, because the lack of constant renovation left park-goers seeking new thrills elsewhere.

In 1902, 70 of the 92 days of summer were cloudy, dismal, and rainy, and Boyton's business nearly went down the drain. He readily accepted a bid to lease his property and pulled the plug on the future of Sea Lion Park.

Steeplechase Park

At the 1893 Chicago Exposition, George Tilyou first saw the Ferris wheel. Upon returning, Tilyou leased a small space on Coney Island and put up a placard that read: "On This Site Will Be Erected The World's Largest Ferris Wheel." He sold enough concession space around the attraction, to pay for the wheel he'd ordered upon delivery in 1894. Although his wheel was actually only 125 feet in diameter consisting of 12 cars that held 18 passengers each—about half the size of the original spectacle—he decorated it with hundreds of

The Steeplechase ride

Steeplechase Park's namesake was a large, elaborate mechanical horse-racing ride. Commissioned by George Tilyou in 1897, the original ride was destroyed by a 1907 fire and rebuilt. The Steeplechase was in essence an eight-track racing coaster with individual cars in the shape of horses. The famous ride, part of which is shown next to Steeplechase's Pavilion of Fun at right, survived the park's closing in 1964 and was purchased by a Florida park where it was reassembled and operated. When that park closed, the Steeplechase ride was dismantled and reportedly shipped back to an undisclosed storage location in New York. AUTHOR'S COLLECTION

Luna Park, Coney Island, 1903

Electricity—the new wonder of the nineteenth century—transformed Luna Park into an enchanting, mystical wonderland at night. Since fluorescent and neon lighting (both staples of latter-day parks) were still years off, all illumination at Luna was by incandescent bulbs—250,000 of them. When Dreamland opened a year later, boasting one million lights, the glow could be seen for miles, earning Coney the nickname "City of Fire."

luminous lights and it became the most popular sensation of Coney Island.

In the wake of Sea Lion Park's initial success (at least in terms of popularity with the public), Tilyou decided to build an enclosed park. Since horse racing was well loved on Coney, Tilyou predicted that a similar amusement ride would be well received. Following the model of a British-originated mechanical racetrack, Tilyou brought in the *Steeplechase* ride. Eight wooden horses dashed the length of a swaggering curved metal track and offered potential jockeys

an extremely realistic horse-racing experience.

When Steeplechase Park opened in the spring of 1897, admission was 25 cents, and that bought customers a wide array of exciting new thrills and adventures. He surrounded his Ferris wheel with a ride called the *Intramural Bicycle Railway*, as well as an elevated corkscrew slide, a carousel, and a *Scenic Railway*.

George Tilyou knew that ever-changing amusements would be the key to success, so he kept his ear to the ground to bring the latest and greatest to Steeplechase Park. On a scouting trip to

Buffalo's 1901 Pan American Exposition, he spied an until then unseen illusion ride called *A Trip to the Moon* owned by Frederic W. Thompson. Tilyou offered Thompson and his partner Elmer "Skip" Dundy 60 per cent of net profits to bring the ingenious ride to Steeplechase. Since it wasn't slotted to perform anywhere until the St. Louis Exposition in 1904, the partners eagerly agreed.

A spaceship with flapping wings was located in the center of a large, round building, boarded by thirty passengers who peered out through portholes. Following the captain's countdown, projections against the walls provided the illusions of a blastoff from the fairgrounds, passage over Niagara Falls, and penetration into space. The spaceship itself heaved and swayed to promote the sensation of motion. Viewers watched the earth's surface shrink in the distance and approached the heretofore unimaginable moon, complete with craters, canyons, and prairies. Having "landed" and disembarked, the passengers were guided through underground passageways and caverns populated with giants and dwarfs, and led eventually to a grotto where the Man in the Moon sat on a royal throne, encircled by a harem of dancing moon maidens. The spectacle ended when the passengers crossed over an unsteadily swaying bridge and returned to the

Entrance to Luna Park, Coney Island, N.Y.

16814   114

startling reality of the park. The result was an overwhelmingly complete audio-visual and physical illusion that convinced many people that they had in fact traveled through space.

Thompson, an architectural student, and Dundy, the showman, brought two other attractions to Steeplechase that year. The *Darkness*

Helter Skelter slide at Luna Park
The simple thrill provided by this swaggering slide—called the Helter Skelter—at Coney's Luna Park provided a quick way down from the elevated promenade. It was just the kind of entertainment that folks enjoyed during the easy-going years of the early twentieth century. AUTHOR'S COLLECTION

The Tickler, Luna Park
One of the more daring rides of the era was the Tickler, in which passengers rode a free-wheeling tub on casters. After being hoisted to the top of the ride (the lift hill is partially visible in the background), the cars rolled and zigzagged back to the bottom, pinball style. AUTHOR'S COLLECTION

and Dawn was another illusion cyclorama and the *Aerio Cycle* (called the *Giant SeeSaw* at Steeplechase) a great elaboration on the original pleasure wheel. In this case, two small Ferris wheels were mounted on either end of an enormous teeter, which lifted passengers 235 feet into the Coney Island sky for a breathtaking view of the attractions and New York City.

Luna Park

The coinciding conclusions of business at Sea Lion Park and the lease agreement between George Tilyou, Frederic Thompson, and Elmer Dundy resulted in Luna Park. Thompson and Dundy bought additional acres and imported *A Trip to the Moon* from Steeplechase Park. Except for the *Shoot-the-Chutes*, they razed and buried Sea Lion Park in amusement park history. Some say it was named for Dundy's sister, Luna, but advertising makes clear the new amusement extravaganza was the namesake of the airship *Luna*.

In November of 1902 a labor force of 700, including illusionists, artisans, artists, inventors, painters, carpenters, electricians, and blacksmiths began to work around the clock to turn Frederic Thompson's visions of elegance and exotic into a reality on Coney Island.

The central Promenade and its elevated walkway were the main thoroughfare and a visual smorgasbord. Instead of the traditional lone central tower common to parks, Thompson peppered their acreage with hundreds of turrets, spires, and minarets that offered novel and nostalgic views to New Yorkers of all ages. It was foreign and picturesque during the day, but when a quarter of a million lights were powered up at the grand opening on May 16, 1903, the effect was of a sparkling, enchanted fairyland. The admission fee was ten cents: beautiful female ticket venders stood on Roman chariots in fancy evening attire, and when they ran out of change they let people in free of charge. Within a couple of hours over 43,000 visitors were in attendance and the first day's tally would exceed 60,000.

Thompson understood amusement park patrons. He said: "The keynote of the thing they do demand is change. Everything must be different from ordinary experience. What is presented to them must have life action, motion, sensation, surprise, shock, swiftness, or else comedy."

To appease these demands, Luna Park offered myriad attractions. To the right they saw a Venetian city with detailed facades and colonnades complete with a canal crossed by an illuminated bridge and swarming with rowing gondoliers. Flanking the canal, hand-cranked "mutoscopes" churned a drum of flip card pictures and allowed people to view a selection of miniature movies for a penny.

To the left was *A Trip to the Moon* in a new building that cost $52,000 to construct. The new ride's center adornment, *Luna III*, accommodated more passengers than the original. Oversized wings flapped on either side of the ride, and gimbaled bearings provided a realistic rocking motion. In another alteration from the original ride, passengers were led into the mouth of a dragon and through its dark, clammy, fluctuating stomach before being expelled back earth and Luna Park.

Fort Hamilton and New York Bay were replicated in the War of the Worlds building where a dazzling miniature version of the allied armies of Europe mounted for an attack. Admiral Dewey's fleet eventually sank every one of the French, German, Spanish, and British ships using a mixture of actors and electrically controlled models as the spectators and a lifelike copy of the Statue of Liberty looked on.

Beyond this theater of war, a building housed Luna's *Twenty Thousand Leagues Under the Sea*, a submarine ride that took passengers to the polar regions. Lured in by an Eskimo barker donned in fur, visitors saw slimy, slithering seaweed and octopi, strange oceanic creatures, and a mermaid. Real seals and polar bears inhabited the icebergs and an igloo and sleds powered by dog teams were kept at a chilling temperature by a huge refrigeration plant.

Farther out along the Court of Honor, the bright lights of the *Shoot-the-Chutes* and the Electric Tower decorated the horizon visible from miles

around. Not far from the *Shoot-the-Chutes* stood a unique exhibit indeed. Dr. Courney's Baby Incubator displayed premature babies ribboned in blue or pink that were tended to by wet nurses.

In other sections of the park, visitors could find a Chinese theater; villages of German, Irish Hindu, and Eskimo origin; Japanese gardens; a miniature railroad with a locomotive larger than its engineer; and Wormwood's Monkey Theater—plus dancing and swimming facilities.

As partners and businessmen, Thompson and Dundy made a powerful impact on the amusement park industry. Their combined prowess in showmanship and strategy, balancing thrilling rides for tickets with extravagant free entertainment productions, entertained first-time patrons and repeat customers equally. Luna Park was a phenomenal success.

Among the spectacles that amused the throngs were a performance of elephants sliding down the *Shoot-the-Chutes* into the lagoon below; a lifelike replication called the *Streets of Delhi*, which took visitors to the other side of the globe; and *Fire and Flames*. Hundreds of firefighters battled real (but controlled) flames that threatened a four-story building and a rescue squad saved occupants from the building's upper floors.

Luna continued to prosper through the early part of the twentieth century, thriving on Thompson and Dundy's successful formula of ever-changing rides and visual productions.

Skip Dundy died suddenly in 1907 and left Thompson to his own devices, which included heavy drinking and promoting his new wife as an actress. The park continued draw to crowds through a change in ownership in 1912.

Barron Collier, a former advertising expert, took over when Thompson had run up excessive debts and lost his fire insurance coverage. He

Riding the Elephant at Coney Island, N. Y.

70-69

Baby elephant walk

With America's longtime fascination for things zoological, wild animals were always a popular attraction at amusement establishments. In this World War I-era view, a trained elephant provides a lofty—if undulating—tour of Coney Island.
AUTHOR'S COLLECTION

SHOOTING THE CHUTES,
DREAMLAND,

CONEY ISLAND, N.Y.

Dreamland, Coney Island

Dreamland parroted the highly successful Luna Park in several respects—except for success. Like its mentor park, Dreamland featured architecture from faraway lands, all lit at night with incandescent bulbs—one million of them. One of Dreamland's most popular attractions was the Shoot-the-Chutes ride, which in this heavily retouched photo has been partially dubbed in, in the foreground, by an artist (the view looks down from the top of the chute). The tower was patterned after the Giradela in Seville, Spain.

AUTHOR'S COLLECTION

expanded the park to include 31 buildings for shows, amusements, and 28 rides. A *Turkey Trot*, traveling merry-go-round, and a coal-mine attraction that employed donkeys pulling customers through dark tunnels were a few of the new features. Some 1,500 employees kept the park in operation, which now featured 1,450,000 electric lights, 2,054 towers and minarets, and issued 315 miles of tickets each summer.

World War I and the ensuing interest in war-type thrills brought *Aerial Night Attacks* in 1916, a production that showed miniature German zeppelin attacks on a replica of a French village. Other attractions that joined Luna Park in the war years included Heppe's Kandy Meat Market, which offered confections in the shapes of farm animals and pets; an Alligator Farm; and Darktown Follies, an African-American musical revue. In the 1920s the management tried its hand at

fun-house thrills. Patrons walked in and around a distorted house called *Thru the Falls* and raced along the *Down & Out Slide* and the *Soft Spot*, a figure-8 slide exclusively for children. Games similar to dunk tanks became popular at the same time, sending pigs or people into a tank of water.

When Baron Collier brought in Arthur Jarvis as Luna's general manager, it looked like an administrative coup for the park. Jarvis had been a force in the creation of several of Coney Island's most exciting roller coasters. He brought the well-known *Drop the Dip* coaster from the Bowery to Luna in 1924 and added the *Mile Sky Chaser*. Complete with six drops, some stretching over 70 feet in length, it was Coney's highest and longest roller coaster and had unending lines of anxious passengers every weekend. Over a million people soared over its tracks during its first year of operation.

Rainy seasons and the money-tight depression years hit Coney Island hard. Admission rates were dropped and improvement schedules were minimized, but Luna still went bankrupt in May, 1933. Collier attempted a rally by reopening a few rides and about half the park in 1934, but then cut his losses and sold the park in 1935. It was Coney's ever-threatening nemesis, fire, that eventually put Luna Park out of business in 1944.

Dreamland

In July 1903, two Coney Island lots, 15 acres in all, came up for auction. The sale of these parcels caught the eye of Manhattan real-estate magnate William H. Reynolds, who had been lustfully watching Luna Park and its huge box-office success. Cunningly, Reynolds acquired both pieces of property, and through political manipulation, got the city to grant him not only the street that divided his property, but the old Iron Pier at the end of the street, as well. The significance of this coup was that not only did his property become united, but he cut off free public access to the shoreline.

Architects Kirby, Pettit & Green were given a free hand to design Dreamland from scratch, so they capitalized on the beach front location and laid out wide avenues around a central lagoon that offered scenic views, refreshing breezes, and a salt water flow from the open gates at high tide. Compared with the dazzling chaos of Luna Park, Dreamland was a composition of harmony. Working toward a May 15, 1904, opening, thousands of carpenters, masons, and iron workers began in December to raise buildings of artificial stone, install 1,700 tons of asbestos fireproofing, and construct a 600,000 gallon central water tower.

Dreamland's owners planned a display of grandeur in its natural and architectural beauty. The horseshoe shaped lagoon was traversed by a pedestrian bridge and circumscribed by the elaborate promenades and attractions that were coated with gleaming white paint for opening day. A replica of Spain's Giradela Tower, the 375-foot tall Beacon Tower was festooned with 100,000 lights on a pure white background and broadcast the emergence of the new park to the Coney Island scene. Just beyond the main entrance, visitors were greeted by a Grecian-style arena topped with statues of trumpeting elephants acting as silent barkers to announce Bostock's Circus. Many acts were featured in the building over the years, including Madame

Aurora and her polar bears; Herman Weedom and his rag-tag collection of trained hyenas, tigers, leopards, and lions; but the main act of the three-ring circus was the ever-popular Captain Bonavita and his troupe of lions.

None of the original authors of Dreamland were of show-business stock, so they hired Samuel Gumpertz to bring in the entertainment element. With a personal resume that featured circus, theater, and rodeo stints, he proposed one of the most unique attractions of Coney Island's history: *Liliputia*—a half-scale midget village modeled on fifteenth century Nuremburg and hundreds of inhabitants, who would live there and entertain the paying public. The complete community included everything proportional to the residents: tiny lifeguards manning diminutive towers at the beach. Their parliament enacted little laws, and a miniature operational livery was stocked with horses; diminutive Chinese laundrymen charged small rates for small suits, pressed and starched. Occasionally a "giant" was sent in to walk the village, accentuating the scale of the people, their homes and pets.

Ben Morris and his Wonderful Illusions presented dazzling magic acts from London and Paris, including a hypnotized girl named Ariel, who floated above the heads of the audience.

Dreamland Circus, Coney Island

Around 2 A.M. on May 27, 1911, Dreamland's Hell Gate attraction was in flames. By 3 A.M., Dreamland was a double-nine-alarm fire, and Coney Island was once again literally a city of fire. By dawn, the fire was out, but Dreamland had completely disappeared. Dreamland's manager, Samuel Gumpertz, proclaimied that Dreamland would rise from the ashes. Ultimately, all that would rise was Gumbertz's freak show—fancy by side-show standards, but not much of a reminder of Dreamland. Gumbertz's elaborate new attraction was located on Surf Avenue. Like the original Dreamland freak show, his rebuilt attraction contained a large number of freaks and other interesting phenomenon gathered from all parts of the world.
AUTHOR'S COLLECTION

Dreamland Circus, Coney Island, N. Y.

Nathan's Famous Frankfurters
Not to dine at Nathan's is not to see Coney Island. This cuisinary citadel is yet another landmark at the world's most famous amusement area. People from all walks of life crowd the counters at Nathan's on a June afternoon in 1980 for a world-famous hot dog. But you might want to save your dog eating until _after_ your ride on the nearby Cyclone. MIKE SCHAFER

Another production, "Our Boys in Blue," paid tribute to the army. Wormwood's "Dog and Monkey Show," a tour of the "Swiss Alps", an opportunity to angle for money by hooking a mechanical tin fish, a Japanese teahouse, and the _Haunted Swing_ were other attractions offered on the promenades.

If Dreamland was originally designed to outdo Luna, its architects rose to the occasion. Twin, adjacent _Shoot-the-Chutes_, with a capacity of 7,000 riders an hour, was the largest water slide ever constructed. A single production of "Fighting the Flames" involved a cast of 2,000: 120 firefighters employing four engines, hose wagons, and an extension-ladder truck at a six-story hotel somewhat shamed the smaller version staged at Luna.

The aim for novelties did not completely overtake the creators of Dreamland. In fact, six attractions, including Dr. Courtney and his incubation babies, moved directly across Surf Avenue from Luna Park. It was clearly a park designed to live up to its name, as Dreamland's rides focused on transporting the public to real and fantasy places far from the shores of Coney Island. To an extreme, the 1904 season took riders to the underworld on _Hell Gate_. A 50-foot whirlpool pulled boats into ever narrowing circles until they eventually disappeared before the eyes of hundreds of

astonished spectators. An iron and wood channel, beyond the scope of the fearful, took passengers into a journey "beneath" the surface of the earth, through plaster of Paris caverns of "Hell."

Ironically, this ride would lead directly to the end of Dreamland's existence. Before opening weekend in 1911, tinsmiths worked past midnight to fix a leak in the water flume with hot tar. A cluster of lights illuminating the work exploded around 1:30 A.M.—the result of a faulty circuit or the heat from the tar. Workers found themselves stranded in darkness. A bucket of hot tar was accidentally kicked over and a within minutes _Hell Gate_ was aflame. That ride was overtaken by flames and sparks flew to the flimsily constructed facades of nearby attractions. Real firefighters fought the real threat to the park for several hours.

During the struggle, a huge panic ensued, as water pressure failed, animals attempted to flee, and rescue efforts were foiled by uncooperative elephants while wind blew the sparks inland.

Ultimately, all 15 acres of Dreamland were reduced to smoking ruins, along with almost as much property on either side of it. Since insurance covered only a fraction of the $2.2 million worth of damages, Dreamland was not rebuilt.

The Nickel Empire

1920 brought New York's subway system to Coney Island, delivering the throngs at a nickel apiece. Thus, the "Nickel Empire" was born. A nickel bought you a hot dog, a milkshake, or a spin on most of the rides. Nathan's flourished. The rides got wilder.

In 1920, the _Wonder Wheel_ was built, and later the _Bobs_ (eventually renamed the _Tornado_), _Thunderbolt_, and _Cyclone_ roller coasters. The Roaring Twenties also brought the Boardwalk. Eighty feet wide and two miles long, above or below, it became a popular place for couples to court.

The new arrivals to Coney Island were a different class of people. Past visitors had been first the upper, then the middle and working classes, but this new group were mostly recent immigrants, largely New York's working poor. They came by subway with nickels in their pockets, food in their picnic baskets, and bathing attire under their street clothes. Although they couldn't afford the standard attractions, new ones, like "guess men" and side shows, sprang up to separate them from their nickels.

The change this brought to Coney Island was remarkable. At the turn of the twentieth century,

Astroland and Deno's Wonder Wheel Park, Coney Island
The width and breadth of amusement attractions at Coney Island have been severely curtailed, but it's still a great place to spend a summer day. The main park today is Astroland, shown, along with Deno's Wonder Wheel Park (a tiny operation surrounded by Astroland) in a 1983 view that looks northeasterly. A landmark at Coney since 1920, Wonder Wheel, with its inner wheel of cabins that fling outward as the wheel rotates, dominates the landscape, along with the world-famous Cyclone, partially visible in the distance. BOTH PHOTOS, OTTO P. DOBNICK

Parachute Jump, Coney Island

Steeplechase Park's Parachute Jump was a holdover from the 1940 New York World's Fair. Although the ride has not functioned since the original Steeplechase closed in 1964, its superstructure stands as a silent sentinel of happier times at America's Playground. OTTO P. DOBNICK COLLECTION

The Cyclone

People come from all over the world to experience one of the most famous roller coasters in the world, the Coney Island Cyclone, shown in 1983. Although now considered part of Astroland, it occupies its own site at Surf and 10th just west of the New York Aquarium. OTTO P. DOBNICK

an average summer Sunday would welcome 100,000 visitors to Coney and by the 1920s weekend crowds topped a million sun-seekers in a single day. With such a large potential audience, every showman, carnival man, and con-man in the country headed for Coney Island. The concentration of rides, games, grab-joints, souvenir stands, shooting galleries, arcades, and sideshows that proliferated on this thin strip of sand was staggering. Of course, every attraction had a barker, and every barker a spiel or ballyhoo. Coney Island, that great City of Fire that had delighted the eye a decade earlier, was instead assaulting the ear.

The Great Depression of the 1930s couldn't even slow the Nickel Empire. Indeed, the need for cheap diversion only grew.

173   Parachute Jump, Coney Island, N. Y.

Coney's carousel
It's no longer a nickel, but you can still take a spin on Coney Island's beautiful carousel, housed in its own building. OTTO P. DOBNICK

Modern Coney

The end of an era came in the late 1930s when Coney Island (at least the beach and boardwalk) came under the jurisdiction of New York's Parks Department commissioner Robert Moses. Moses hated Coney and set about to clean it up. The barkers were told to shut up or face arrest. As the din diminished, so did the crowds. The 1940s saw good business at Coney, but with the loss of Luna Park, Steeplechase became the last of the great Coney Island parks, and the only real unifying force on the beach. When it closed in 1964, it looked like Coney was indeed dead.

Fortunately, a new park called Astroland stepped up to carry the torch. In 1969, when the *Cyclone* roller coaster was condemned by the City of New York and slated for demolition for parking-lot expansion for the neighboring aquarium, it was Astroland that ultimately stepped in. By saving, refurbishing, and reopening the venerable *Cyclone*, Astroland ensured that the 1927-built coaster would entertain a new generation of thrill-seekers. As it turned out, Astroland saved what in the year 2001 would be the only remaining wood-tracked coaster to grace the shores of this once great amusement empire. In 2000, the *Thunderbolt* coaster—a sister ride to the *Cyclone* that had been standing moribund since the 1980s

(the *Thunderbolt* is perhaps best known for its use as a prop in the Woody Allen movie *Annie Hall*) —was leveled.

Astroland was joined by Deno's Wonder Wheel Park and a small gathering of rides called Steeplechase Park, bearing little connection to the original. The only remaining tribute to the era of the great parks, aside from *Wonder Wheel* and the *Cyclone*, is the structure of the *Parachute Drop*. Moved to the original Steeplechase in 1941 after its appearance at the New York World's Fair, it has been refurbished by the City of New York as a static landmark to remind us of Coney's thriving past.

Shrunken to its current size and aging somewhat ungracefully, Coney Island's amusement area continues to be a vibrant place during the summer season. The *Cyclone*, still one of the best and most-well-known roller coasters in the world, continues to be the benchmark by which all other coasters are judged and is Coney's greatest draw (more non-New Yorkers are probably aware of the *Cyclone* than of adjacent New York Aquarium) during the tourist season. Nathan's Famous continues to serve what many believe to be the best hot dog in the world. And, a ride on the *Wonder Wheel* is as frightening as ever. Despite rumors to the contrary, Coney Island is alive and generally well. For now.

Municipal and La Monica piers, Santa Monica, California

A fabulous amusement area developed on Santa Monica Bay on the Pacific Coast near Los Angeles during the early years of the twentieth century. Despite the ravages of weather and fires, several amusement piers and boardwalks flourished at Santa Monica and nearby Venice. This is the Santa Monica Pleasure Pier during the 1920s when its premier ride was the Whirlwind Dipper roller coaster, created by the ride-building team of Thomas Prior and Fred Church. Prior & Church designed and built a number of rides at a number of piers on Santa Monica Bay. MIKE SCHAFER COLLECTION

Luna Park, Pittsburgh, Pennsylvania

FACING PAGE: Inspired by the Coney Island itself as well as the individual parks at Coney Island—notably Luna Park, Dreamland, and Steeplechase—parks that popped up elsewhere in America often blatantly copied the names of the originals, and sometimes their design, too. AUTHOR'S COLLECTION

3 AN IDEA SPREADS
From Atlantic to Pacific

Seaside piers, trolley parks, and copycats

With the turn of the twentieth century, the stage was set for the rapid national spread of amusement parks. America was ready to play, and there were people and machines ready to help her. There were three distinct influences on this growth: the natural draw of the seashore; electric railway companies' desire for weekend revenue; and the ability and willingness to quickly replicate a proven success.

Architecture was an important part of the amusement park experience at this point. Luna and Dreamland at New York's Coney Island set the standard, while Frederick

Ingersoll—a roller coaster- and ride-builder from Pittsburgh—and others carried the trend across the country. Electric railway companies that built their own parks generally used whatever architectural and engineering talent they had at their disposal, within their own ranks, and limited capital often kept them from creating anything nearly as elaborate as Dreamland and Luna. But as electric streetcar and interurban ("traction") companies divested themselves of parks, selling them to private concerns or to new companies that specialized in entertainment, the character of amusement park design changed. In the case of smaller parks, particularly in smaller cities, parks often grew slowly out of a picnic grove or municipal park. These parks usually grew a ride at a time with the only consideration, from a design standpoint, being where to put the next ride. Whatever the design considerations, most of the inland parks were organized as a cohesive entity with a single name, such as Playland or Lakeside. The seaside amusements, however, with rare exception, were built on piers or boardwalks with individual attractions leasing space. This approach allowed for the most rapid growth, but offered little assurance of longevity, and most have disappeared.

Down by the seashore

It seems to be an unwritten law that a traditional amusement park just had to be located next to a body of water. Along America's sea and gulf coasts, the natural draw of the sun and beach made for an irresistible place to locate these new attractions. By the time Coney Island was in full swing, all of America's coasts were dotted with amusement resorts of all kinds.

THE RAZZLE-DAZZLE STEEPLECHASE. FUNNY PLACE STEEPLECHASE ATLANTIC CITY, N. J.

Razzle-Dazzle at Atlantic City

Apparently without the benefit of any kind of safety harnesses, riders brave the undulating Razzle-Dazzle ride on the Steeplechase Pier at Atlantic City in this postcard postmarked 1917. Blatantly copying the more famous Steeplechase several miles north, this pier even referred to itself as "the Funny Place." AUTHOR'S COLLECTION

Loop the Loop, Atlantic City

Coney Island did not hold a monopoly on sporting the first looping coasters. First there was the Flip-Flap with its round loop; then the Loop the Loop's eliptical loop. Lina Beecher then built this eliptical loop at Atlantic City, New Jersey, but lack of capacity was still its downfuall. AUTHOR'S COLLECTION

ATLANTIC CITY

Although the resort at Long Branch, New Jersey, is considered to be the first amusement area on the Jersey Shore, one of the most famous amusement areas in all of America, outside of Coney Island, was Atlantic City. Sporting seven entertainment piers by 1913, it became known as the "Queen of Resorts."

Atlantic City came into existence in the mid-1800s and was the brainchild of Dr. Jonathan Pitney, an early director of Atlantic County. His inspired idea of a spa-by-the-sea included a railroad to transport people from Philadelphia. Philadelphia civil engineer Richard B. Osborne helped plan the new resort destination and is credited with christening it "Atlantic City." On July 1, 1854, the first passenger trains rumbled out of Camden, New Jersey, for the new seashore destination, filled with passengers ferried across the Delaware River from Philadelphia. The incoming tide frothed with money, enthusiasm, and optimism. Dr. Pitney soon became known as the "Father of Atlantic City."

Atlantic City's soon-to-be famous Boardwalk opened on June 26, 1870. Designed to keep the sand off the hotel carpets and railroad car seats, the mile-long wooden walkway was the world's first. From the Boardwalk would spring various amusement rides and whole amusement piers that would further foster Atlantic City's reputation. In 1887, for instance, La Marcus A. Thompson—the "father of the roller coaster"—opened the first "scenic railway" coaster on the Boardwalk, between Tennessee and New York avenues.

Although not the first, Steel Pier, which opened in 1898, was the most popular venue for entertainment on the Atlantic City Boardwalk for 81 years. Top performers in vaudeville, comedy, and music performed there, and audiences came dressed to the nines, proud to be seen at the "Showplace of the Nation." One of Steel Pier's biggest rivals was the 700-foot Garden Pier, opened in 1913. It had some 25 stores, a courtyard flanked by pavilions, and a four-towered edifice complete with ballroom, theater, and exhibition hall. Marquees boasted novelties like indoor golf and a children's carnival. Flags rippled atop the Keith Theatre's four steeples and terra cotta roof as striped awnings shaded arched entranceways below. The nineteenth-century-style ambiance was complete—the ramp that guided Packards and Hudsons to the sub-boardwalk parking notwithstanding.

Perhaps best-known of the amusement-park-type operations in Atlantic City was Steeplechase Pier, which borrowed the name, of course, from its more famous counterpart 100 miles to the north. Another well-known pier was the Million Dollar Pier, whose name would be copied on a famous amusement park pier on the West Coast.

Most of the piers in Atlantic City are now gone. The business of amusement here has shifted toward new casinos after gambling was legalized in 1978 while the more traditional amusements moved southward on the Jersey shore.

WILDWOOD, NEW JERSEY

Wildwood is a seashore town with a mobile history: the beach and the great amusement rides that spin skyward; the frenetic midway; and the energetic visitors. It all began with Wildwood's boardwalk. Primitive walkways began to appear in 1890 as shopkeepers and hotel owners built temporary structures that could be removed and stored during the winter months. By the turn of the century, the area's increasing foot traffic persuaded municipal leaders to invest in a boardwalk along Atlantic Avenue, and it was built.

Boardwalk, Wildwood, New Jersey

Like Coney Island, Atlantic City, and other seashore amusement areas, Wildwood sports a boardwalk that links its various piers—Wild Wheels, Mariner's Landing, and Morey's Pier—along the ocean front. In true boardwalk fashion, the wooden walkway is crammed with eateries, T-shirt shops, and arcades. In 1998, a tram cruised the two-mile boardwalk. OTTO P. DOBNICK

Then, a newer, elevated boardwalk was built east of Atlantic Avenue, closer to the ocean, in 1904. Soon after, North Wildwood and Holly Beach built boardwalks connected to that of Wildwood's, providing a continuous, two-and-a-half-mile promenade. With the new Ocean Pier extending to the Wildwood surf, the resort was presenting Atlantic City with a challenge for summer tourists. Stores, eateries, and amusements appeared and flourished on "the boards."

Due to the coastline's mysterious littoral drift, with sands carried in from the north on coastal currents, the beach continued to swell, putting the boardwalk farther from the lapping ocean waves. In Wildwood, this resulted in some salty political strife when it was proposed to relocate the boardwalk closer to the ocean—a move which would have left a number of retail owners and amusement operators high and dry.

Finally, at 12:01 A.M. on a Sunday morning in 1920, the ocean's quiet rhythm played background music to the sounds of splintering wood as municipal orders compelled workers to dismantle an eight-block stretch of the boardwalk. City Commissioner Oliver Bright led the nocturnal charge, which was planned to elude the long arm of the law (local judges didn't work on Sunday). The wrecking crew worked through the night, hammering away so that by sunrise the demolition was complete.

Commissioner Bright's objective was financial; he intended to bolster sagging city coffers by

pushing the boardwalk oceanward and creating a new generation of taxable lots. A real-estate monger himself, Bright would likewise benefit from the expansion of Wildwood. The Bright initiative, in effect, would force everyone's hand and end the squabbling.

The business community relented, and the city proceeded to relocate the great wooden way. By August 1921, the new, oceanward boardwalk was connected to the remains of its predecessor by a right-angled spur at Montgomery Avenue. Nonetheless, Commissioner Bright lost the next election.

In the years that followed, rescue and repair crews would battle fires, hurricanes, and a stray lion, but the boardwalk maintained its position as the gateway to Wildwood's entertainment. The Big Bands played there, with band leaders like Duke Ellington and a host of otherwell-known marquee names. Animal acts were popular attractions until 1938 when a lion named Tuffy escaped, joined the boardwalk throngs, and killed a man.

Mariner's Landing Pier, Wildwood

This 1989 view from the Big Wheel at Mariner's Landing shows an assortment of rides on just one of the four amusement piers at Wildwood. In the foreground is the Sea Serpent roller coaster, Vekoma's first American installation of a "boomerang"-type coaster. Note the expanse of beach in the background. The amusement piers are huge, but they come nowhere near the water's edge.

With World War II came a reduced boardwalk dazzle, and the hurricane of '44 wreaked havoc, but the 1950s heralded in a new era of seashore fun. The Wildwood boardwalk—a stationary swath of wooden planks and a world of perpetual motion—continues to host game booths, rides with great wheels revolving against the sky, and brand-new, breathless roller coasters. Near the boards, another dynamic body exerts influence in Wildwood: the beach. It continues to grow, now extending nearly a half-mile to water's edge, with an almost unlimited capacity for sailboat races, marbles tournaments, and concerts-by-the-sea. (Taking in the thinning strands at Atlantic City, people sometimes say, "Atlantic City's beach is in Wildwood"—not literally, but the image is accurate.)

UP AND DOWN THE EAST COAST

While New Jersey drew from a large middle Atlantic population, many other areas along the Atlantic seaboard were popular as well. Ocean City, Maryland, still has an amusement area, but Ocean View Park—which played a starring role in the 1977 movie *Rollercoaster*—and Buckroe Beach on the Virginia coast disappeared in the 1970s and 1980s. South Carolina's Myrtle Beach continues to be a tourist destination that supports several amusement parks. Florida, a state with a long and colorful amusement history, still has a couple of small seaside parks and a gem on the Gulf side at Panama City known as the Miracle Strip. However, Texas, which once had a couple great traditional Gulf Coast parks, has seen the amusement concept migrate inland as theme parks. Even New England, once home to no less than ten significant amusement areas like Revere Beach, Massachusetts, now has little in the way of coastal amusements. In fact, the only great coastal park of yore left north of Coney Island is in nearby Westchester County, New York.

Miracle Strip, Panama City, Florida

Among the few remaining Gulf Coast amusement areas, the Miracle Strip at Panama City offers a selection of classic rides and attractions, right at beach side. The Starliner coaster looms over the amusement park and the white-sand beach area in this scene from 1987. OTTO P. DOBNICK

Old Orchard Beach, Maine

Once a major amusement area on Saco Bay south of Portland, Old Orchard Beach could be considered the Coney Island of New England. Though still a popular beach resort, its amusement area has diminished over the years, although a new park, Funtown U.S.A., has opened nearby. AUTHOR'S COLLECTION

Savin Rock, Connecticut

Serving the New Haven area beginning in the 1830s, Savin Rock had competing amusement piers, one of which was home to the fearsome Thunderbolt coaster, built in 1925. AUTHOR'S COLLECTION

Westward ho

As the population of America moved west, it carried with it the idea of amusement centers. And like the development of Coney Island, a few people with great forethought took real-estate chances and invested their money in fulfilling the general population's desire for fun and thrills at the beach. Oceanside parks quickly spread from San Diego, California, to Seattle, Washington. The California coast was once dotted with amusements at Mission Beach (San Diego); Long Beach, Ocean Beach, Seal Beach, Redondo Beach, Venice, Ocean Park, and Santa Monica in the Los Angeles area; Santa Cruz, and San Francisco. Although the new Pacific Park resides on the old Santa Monica pier, and Belmont Park at Mission Beach has been reborn on a limited scale, Santa Cruz has the only remaining traditional seaside amusement park on the West Coast.

SEASIDE IN SOUTHERN CALIFORNIA

Nowhere on the California coast was the amusement park business as intense as it was in the Los Angeles area, particularly Santa Monica and nearby Venice. The history of parks and their related ocean piers on Santa Monica Bay is quite convoluted, punctuated by politics and—the bane of amusement parks everywhere—ravaging fires.

Of the numerous personages and companies involved in the amusement history of this area, one man stands above most others: Abbot Kinney. A tobacco tycoon inspired by the area's intoxicating weather, Kinney and his partner

Francis Ryan acquired a controlling interest in the Ocean Park Casino at Santa Monica in June 1891. Several months later they bought the surrounding tract of land, including a swath of real estate extending 1½ miles south into Venice.

They quickly realized that the success of their new beach resort was dependent on reliable, inexpensive, and direct rail service from Los Angeles. Kinney persuaded the Santa Fe Railway to build a branch to Venice and donated 12 acres for its right-of-way into town. The first train arrived on June 18, 1892. In 1896, interurban electric railway Los Angeles Pacific arrived at Santa Monica, further nurturing area growth.

The year 1898 was particularly successful for the community within Santa Monica now known as Ocean Park. Kinney and his partner opened a 40-acre racetrack and golf links near their Casino Country Club at the southern end of the property, and also constructed new commercial buildings as well as 40 beach cottages.

On June 30, 1898, the city of Santa Monica granted Kinney and Ryan permission to use the pilings at Pier Avenue, which then carried a 200-foot-long outfall sewer, to support a new 1,250-foot-long pleasure pier for tourists and fishermen. The project was completed in less than six weeks.

Francis Ryan died after a sudden heart attack in October 1898, after which Kinney had to deal with new business partners. One point of contention between them was how to develop the wetlands on the southern extremity of their property. Eventually, the partners agreed to dissolve their partnership and flip a coin to divide their holdings at a final meeting in January 1904. The coin was tossed high into the tension-filled air; Kinney called "tails" and won, giving him first choice in what portion of property he wanted. "I'll take the salt marshes," he said. His ex-partners were floored—and relieved. They thought the marshes were worthless.

Always a dreamer, Kinney envisioned a "Venice of America"—a slice of Italy in California—to rise on the site. Kinney immediately began to plan his new beach resort with help from hired experts and inspiration from Daniel Burnham's "City Beautiful" movement featured at the World's Columbian Exposition in Chicago in 1893. Venice was to be a planned community whose signature feature was a network of canals like its Italian namesake. In addition, Kinney would build a 900-foot ocean pier for amusement purposes, a 2,000-seat amphitheater, and an ornate bathhouse on a central lagoon that would serve as an enormous saltwater swimming area for 5,000 people. As the pier was being constructed, the Los Angeles Pacific (a future component of the fabled Pacific Electric interurban system) finished its "Short Line" route to Venice, bringing direct trolley service from downtown Los Angeles.

Unfortunately, Kinney's ambition and determination were beaten back by winter ocean storms in 1905. A March tempest brought three-story-high waves, demolishing the new pier and auditorium, eroding the beach, and flooding the entire construction site. Ironically, drifting piles from storm-ravaged recreational piers built by Kinney's ex-partners at nearby Ocean Park caused much of the destruction. Venice Pier was nearly obliterated overnight.

Rebuilding the pier became a top priority. Kinney's 24-hour-a-day labor force was expanded from 600 to 1,000, and by the middle of June the amphitheater and the beachfront structures were almost finished. Finally at 2 P.M. on Friday, June 30, 1904, the battalion of laborers paused momentarily to witness an historical event: As the tide rose, Mrs. Abbott Kinney turned the valve on the pipes that led to the Pacific, allowing salt water to flow in—at some 500 gallons per minute—and fill the swimming lagoon and completed canal segments. In July 1904, newspapers announced that

Piers at Santa Monica Bay, California

This aerial looking north along Santa Monica Bay in 1930 shows the relative proximity of some of the piers that at the time were popular amusement spots. The upper pier is actually two piers: Ocean Park and the adjacent Lick pier at Santa Monica. The major pier this side of it is the famous Abbot Kinney Pier, with its Ship Cafe, Flying Circus, and Giant Dipper roller coaster visible. The small pier in the foreground is the Center Street Pier, on which once stood the Sunset Ballroom. COURTESY JEFFREY STANTON

Venice was open and operating, although it was hardly complete. The Lagoon Bathhouse was not yet ready for business, nor was the miniature railroad that would distribute guests of the Venice Hotel to the amusement areas. Nevertheless, 20,000 people packed Venice streets, piers, and beach each day of the four-day grand-opening celebration. Meanwhile, a huge new bathhouse opened at nearby Ocean Park along with a figure-8-type coaster.

From the start, the Abbot Kinney Pier (sometimes referred to simply as Venice Pier) and the surrounding boardwalk area blossomed in terms of rides and attractions. The Midway Plaisance at the lagoon opened in 1906 as did the Lagoon Bathhouse. By the 1910 season, Venice's first roller coaster appeared, the *Venice Scenic Railroad*, built by L. A. Thompson.

That same year, one of Kinney's former partners, Alexander Fraser, announced that he was

Ocean Park Walk, Venice, California

In this wonderful scene at Fraser Pier early in the twentieth century, the Dragon Gorge Scenic Railroad and its ornate, turretted building (one of the trains is just passing behind the closest turret), dominates the Ocean Park Walk. The white building this side of the Dragon Gorge housed a carousel.
COURTESY JEFFREY STANTON

Venice Scenic Railway and beach

Beaches have forever been a natural draw for people, especially in warm climes. Add other attractions, such as a ballroom, eateries, and thrill rides like the Scenic Railway at Venice Beach, shown early in the twentieth century—and you have a winning combination. AUTHOR'S COLLECTION

The Race Thru The Clouds coaster

Not all rides and attractions were right on the ocean front or on a pier. One of the first major coasters on Santa Monica Bay was The Race Thru The Clouds, which was situated on the south edge of the saltwater lagoon and canals a couple of blocks inland. The twin-track racing coaster, opened in 1911, is shown not long before it was rebuilt with steeper, longer drops in 1921. The entrance area featured several concessions, and the Santa Fe Railway depot was immediately to the right. B. DEREK SHAW COLLECTION

going to build his Million Dollar Pier at adjacent Ocean Park. The 300 x 1,000-foot amusement pier opened in 1911, but Kinney kept up with the competition by adding rides to his empire, including the first racing coaster on the West Coast: *The Race Thru the Clouds*, located not on Kinney's pier but along the swimming lagoon.

Among the Million Dollar Pier's attractions were the 1,000-seat Starland Theater, the *Grand Canyon Electric Railroad* (a rare, third-rail-powered coaster), a Philadelphia Toboggan Company carousel, the Mystic Maze, the *Dragon Gorge* scenic railway, and the famous Infant Incubator demonstrating the newest

techniques in the care of premature babies. For the remainder of the decade, the name of the game was competition between the two big piers as well as with new upstarts, such as Jones Pier, next to Fraser's operation. As the twentieth century's second decade unfolded, the attractions of Santa Monica Bay collectively had become known as "The Coney Island of the Pacific."

Alas, a massive fire on September 3, 1912 wiped out the Million Dollar Pier, but an undeterred Alexander Fraser had it completely rebuilt by the following high season, opening in May 1913. Kinney responded with yet another new racing coaster, the *Derby*. Throughout the rest of the decade, competition—and fire (Ocean Park Pier burned in 1915)—spurred new or updated coasters, flat rides, and attractions.

The year 1920 was pivotal. The Million Dollar Pier, having changed hands, was now known as the Pickering Pleasure Pier, and its new owners expanded it to be the largest amusement pier in the country. On November 4, 1920, Abbot Kinney died, and, in an eerie coincidence, his pier burned to the sand and surf (except for the new *Big Dipper* roller coaster) on December 20, 1920. Heir Thornton Kinney vowed to have the pier rebuilt for the next summer season. By April 15, 1921, the last of the pier pilings was in place and two-thirds of the decking was completed. The rebuilt pier was 1,200 feet long and 525 feet wide; it included an extravagant new dance hall with

The Race thru the Clouds, and Venice Canals, Venice, Cal.

Venice Pier, 1923

Abbot Kinney Pier at Venice, California, burned to the surf in December 1920, but a new pier rose from the ashes. Known also simply as Venice Pier, the rebuilt Abbot Kinney Pier is shown in 1923. At upper right is the famous Ship Cafe, a restaurant built to look like a Spanish galleon. Beyond it are the Giant Dipper and—with the covered lift hill and first drop—Bobs roller coasters. The coaster in the foreground is the unusually named Some Kick. The pier's midway is prominent, top to bottom, at right center in the photo. The striped roof building at center left is the Fun House. COURTESY JEFFREY STANTON

an oval-shaped orchestra pit centered in a 210 x 180-foot hardwood dance floor.

Many of the original ride and concession operators returned to lease space on the new pier. Newer versions of favored rides of the old pier were opened, including the *Over the Falls* mill chute ride, the *Noah's Ark* walk-through, and the *Great American Racing Derby*. Also on the lineup was the new Prior & Church *Bobs* roller coaster, a 60-foot-high ride that featured a tunneled lift hill and first drop into a convoluted track layout.

The new pier cost the Kinney family an estimated $3 million, and $500,000 worth of additional attractions were added two years later, including a $200,000 fun house featuring 25 different types of gag devices, slides, freak shows, and even a kid-size roller coaster that traveled the building perimeter along its rafters. Also debuting in 1923 was the $60,000 *Some Kick* roller coaster, joined in 1924 by Prior & Church's *Giant Dipper* coaster, replacing the *Big Dipper*.

Opened in 1925, the giant landmark *Flying Circus* simulated a genuine stunt-flying experience through six eight-passenger "planes" attached to large, vertical arms suspended from a 65-foot-high rotating central tower. As the planes "flew" around the high tower, bursts of compressed air caused the ride's arms to rise and fall.

The 1920s roared on while dance contests became the highlight of special activities at all the dance halls that lined the beaches. However, late in 1927 Venice began filling in its canals, paving them over to accommodate the booming Automobile Age—much to the protest of many residents. Only a few of the canals remain. In 1929, Ocean Park Pier was expanded again, the lengthened pier crowned by a new *Shoot-the-Chutes* ride—the tallest ever built of this popular series of rides that had first appeared at the original Coney Island in New York in 1895.

The Depression hit Venice's amusement park business immediately, so there were few improvements made during the 1930s. Because money was tight, park managers relied on existing promotions and special celebrations—among them bathing beauty contests, a Halloween carnival, a Christmas Fiesta, and a Mardi Gras—to lure paying customers to their piers. Nonetheless, by 1932, pier business had suffered so significantly that in October the Kinney Company shocked investors and concessionaires alike when it defaulted on bond interest payments. The company was taken over by Edward Gerety Jr.

Pacific Ocean Park

The last hurrah for amusement parks on Santa Monica Bay was Pacific Ocean Park—the result of a heavy makeover of Ocean Park Pier and its surroundings. It featured a nautical theme with space-age touches, as illustrated by the main entrance (RIGHT). The aerial shows the park in 1963. BOTH PHOTOS, AUTHOR'S COLLECTION

Because of their proximity to Hollywood, the piers of Santa Monica Bay were often used in movies that called for a beach or amusement-park settings, such as the memorable scenes in Hal Roach's 1933 "Our Gang" comedy classic, *Fish Hooky*. But laughs were far and few between during the Depression, and the amusement parks of Santa Monica Bay limped along into the 1940s. Pier operations were curtailed at night after the outbreak of World War II, from 1941 to 1943, because any stray light was considered a potential beacon to enemy warships and submarines. Nonetheless, the piers were a popular destination for soldiers and sailors on leave, looking for dancing, music, and women. When the war ended in 1945, Americans anticipated a new prosperity, and the Kinney Company took advantage of the renewed supply of building materials to invest $60,000 into repair work on its deteriorated pier deck.

The company's 25-year tidelands lease for its pier expired on January 13, 1946. Although Venice Pier was back to being a profitable business, with revenues of $100,000 annually, and key to Venice's rebound after the Depression, the City of Los Angeles refused to renew the lease. Ever since Venice had been annexed by Los Angeles, L.A. city officials had vehemently opposed the honky-tonk atmosphere of the amusement area, and this was their chance to eliminate it. An era drew to a close when pier businesses ceased to operate at midnight on Saturday April 20, 1946. Some of the rides were sold to other parks, but the buildings, *Giant Dipper*, *Dragon Slide*, even the huge *Flying Circus* became scrap.

Not under L.A. jurisdiction, Ocean Park Pier survived—barely. Improvements were made and new rides added after World War II, but already the park was feeling the effects of a "new" America, one that would revolve around newfangled television sets and the freedom ushered in by the automobile. The ballroom and Big Band era was over. Ocean Park teetered on, however.

Ironically, L.A. had wiped out the amusement areas of Venice in hopes of improving the liveability of the city, but the opposite happened.

Redondo Beach, California

In the early part of the twentieth century, amusement parks dotted the California coast. This view shows the community of Redondo Beach stretching out behind Prior & Church's Giant Dipper, similar to San Diego's still-operating Giant Dipper coaster at the remains of Belmont Park in San Diego. The Redondo Giant Dipper replaced the Lightning Racer in the mid-1920s and was demolished along with the amusement section in 1933. AUTHOR'S COLLECTION

During the 1950s, Venice degenerated into a haven for motorcycle gangs, drug dealers, and winos. L.A. officials had predicted a rise in real-estate values, but instead they plummeted. L.A. had sucked the lifeblood out of Venice, and revival wouldn't come for another quarter century.

Ocean Park Pier closed at the end of the 1956 season and during the ensuing two years underwent a massive transformation into what became known as Pacific Ocean Park. The $10 million renovation applied a nautical theme to the park, added countless new attractions, and revamped some of the favored older rides, such as the *High Boy* roller coaster, renamed the *Sea Serpent*. New attractions included performing dolphin and seal shows and the *Mystery Island Banana Train* ride, which in Disney-esque fashion took riders on a plantation train through a jungle full of mischievous monkeys and into the bowels of a volcano.

In keeping with the pay-one-price (P.O.P.) format that was beginning to take hold in the amusement industry, Pacific Ocean Park went P.O.P. in 1960, thus reducing the riff-raff and maintaining a family atmosphere—an important consideration in the new era of nuclear families. Alas, Pacific Ocean Park went bankrupt in 1967. The park closed and its rides were auctioned off or demolished, thus ending the colorful history of the amusement parks of Santa Monica Bay.

The people of metro Los Angeles enjoyed several coastal amusement parks beyond those of the Santa Monica area. There were parks at Redondo Beach, Long Beach, Seal Beach and other locations. Most notable of these was The Pike at Long Beach, which is featured as one of the great lost parks in Chapter 7.

In Northern California, two seaside amusement areas served the population's thirst for rides and attractions. In San Francisco during the 1920s, George Whitney—the West Coast's answer to George Tilyou, some might say—built Playland-At-The-Beach, at one time the world's largest privately owned amusement park. Playland clung on until the early 1970s.

The only seaside amusement park on the West Coast that survives in more or less classic form, complete with a wide array of attractions, food, and rides—including one of the best wooden roller coasters anywhere—is the Santa Cruz Beach Boardwalk at Santa Cruz, California. As a survivor, it is featured in Chapter 8.

The trolley parks here

In America, the amusement park and the electric railways came of age about the same time, and their lives were often closely linked. As electric power gained popularity in the late nineteenth century, horse-drawn city railcar lines were rapidly converted to electric power, and street railway ("trolley") systems began to flourish throughout the U.S. and Canada. Soon, nearly every town and city worthy of its name sported at least a single-line trolley operation, used mainly by townsfolk to commute downtown for work or shopping.

Early in the twentieth century the trolley's big cousin, the electric interurban railway, also began to flourish. The distinction between street-railway systems and interurbans is often blurred, the principal difference being that interurban companies linked a series of towns and cities, while a streetcar company usually served but a single metropolitan area. Regardless of their differences, trolley and interurban companies had a common goal: to carry as many passengers as they could, to generate maximum revenues. This goal was easily met on weekdays, but on weekends, most of the trolleys and interurban trains sat idle. Since idle cars do not generate revenues, railway companies took an entrepreneurial approach to the problem by creating destinations to which people could head when they weren't working. A popular solution was to open a picnic grove and extend the railway to it: clear away a few trees, add some picnic tables, tap a well, advertise new weekend schedules to the park, and load up the passengers. Presto! The "electric park" was born.

**Cascade Park,
New Castle, Pennsylvania**

An open-air trolley is just departing the entranceway to Cascade Park in a bygone scene from early in the twentieth century. Countless amusement parks were served by local trolley lines or interurban railways, and in many cases the utility that owned these traction companies themselves built parks as traffic generators. AUTHOR'S COLLECTION

Entrance, Cascade Park, New Castle, Pa.

Starved for interesting diversions, Americans happily embraced the amusement park concept as it burgeoned early in the twentieth century. Trolley and interurban companies were quick to see amusement parks as an even greater draw than picnic parks, and several enterprising companies built their own amusement parks, often with the aid of the parent utility company which owned and operated the trolley or interurban line. But if they didn't build their own park, these companies usually made sure they at least built a line to serve any new park. Regular "steam" railroads also took advantage of parks as a means of handling more passengers. The Bessemer & Lake Erie, primarily an ore-hauling railroad, had a spur off of its Lake Erie-to-Pittsburgh main line at Conneaut, Pennsylvania, that tapped Conneaut Lake Park.

Streetcar and interurban systems were widely popular during the first three decades of the twentieth century, and rare was the amusement park not served by them. Among the many notable examples is Kennywood Park, on the fringes of Pittsburgh. In 1898, the Monongahela Street Railway Company leased a picnic grove—Kenny's Grove—and 141 surrounding acres from Anthony Kenny and set out to create a trolley park. The railway's chief engineer, George Davidson, designed the new park, which was christened Kennywood by Andrew Mellon, founder of the Mellon Bank and later U.S. Secretary of the Treasury. Mellon held an interest in the Monongahela Street Railway, which linked Pittsburgh with the steel mills at Homestead and, beyond Kenny's Grove, at Duquesne (doo-KANE). The park was lit with thousands of electric lights, which cost nothing for the railway to operate. The railroad paid a set charge for electricity, no matter how much it used.

Within a few years of its startup, Kennywood was competing with no fewer than 13 area trolley parks, only one of which remains to this day: Idlewild Park along the Lincoln Highway at Ligonier, Pennsylvania. Interestingly, Kennywood now owns Idlewild.

Saltair on the Great Salt Lake

Steam railroad Salt Lake & Los Angeles built a line west from Salt Lake City on the bed of prehistoric Lake Bonneville, intending to some day reach the West Coast, which it failed to do by a long shot. The railroad was reorganized and rebuilt as an electric interurban railway known as the Salt Lake, Garfield & Western, which built an amusement park on thousands of piles extending into the Great Salt Lake 15 miles west of Salt Lake City. Saltair was known for its huge dance pavilion, which dominates this 1950s view of the park as seen from the lift hill of its defunct racing coaster. SLG&W trains used to come right up to the front door of the pavilion. AUTHOR'S COLLECTION

The Monongahela Street Railway eventually merged with other area trolley lines to form the Pittsburgh Railways Company. PRC divested itself of non-railway enterprises and sold Kennywood to the Pittsburgh & Steeplechase Amusement Company. Pittsburgh's once far-flung streetcar system, which is still partially intact under the guise of Port Authority Transit, brought park-goers right to Kennywood's doorstep until 1958 when the the No. 68 line was converted to buses and streetcars made their final run to Kennywood.

Built on piers over the salty waters of the Great Salt Lake, Saltair was another amusement park built by a railway company. Interurban railway Salt Lake, Garfield & Western linked the 15 miles separating Salt Lake City and the park. Interurban trains operated right up to the park's pavilion via a causeway. The park was SLG&W's principal source of income, but in a bit of a turnabout, the park closed in the late 1950s, while the railroad survived as a local freight switching company, though its line to the Saltair site has long since been abandoned.

Rocky Glen Park at Moosic, Pennsylvania, between Scranton and Wilkes-Barre was built by the Lackawanna & Wyoming Valley interurban railway to serve the people of those two cities,

Whalom Park, Lunenburg, Massachusetts

Whalom Park—here viewed from atop the Ferris wheel—is another trolley park that far outlasted the trolleys. It was opened in 1893 by a traction company based in nearby Fitchburg. The Comet Flyer wooden roller coaster, built in 1938 by the Philadelphia Toboggan Company, serves as Whalom's centerpiece ride. MIKE SCHAFER

Willow Grove Park, Philadelphia

Philadelphia's long-remembered Willow Grove Park once featured a large trolley terminal with many storage tracks, visible in upper center of this colorized scene from circa 1910. Such facilities were necessary for a large park like Willow Grove located in a major American city. Undoubtedly, summer weekends found scores of special trains arriving, crammed with fun-seekers. The trains were stored for the duration of the day or evening until thrilled-out park patrons wearily, but happily, were ready to return home. AUTHOR'S COLLECTION

Entrance to Willow Grove Park, Pa.

65639

situated some 20 miles apart. The third-rail-powered trains of the "Laurel Line," as the L&WV was popularly known, could be seen skirting the park's lake and famous *Million Dollar Coaster*.

In the Midwest, Milwaukeeans rode the big yellow-and-green interurban cars of The Milwaukee Electric Railway & Light Company 20 miles out to Waukesha Beach on Lake Pewaukee to partake of park attractions, including the terrifying *Bobs* roller coaster, a sister ride to the famous *Aeroplane* coaster at Playland in Rye, New York.

The popularity of street railways and interurbans was devastated by a double whammy: the boom in automobile transportation in the 1920s and the Great Depression of the 1930s. By the time of the Depression, many of the railways had sold their parks to companies specializing solely in the entertainment industry, or to private concerns. The Depression brought demise not only to many trolley and interurban lines, but the parks they served. Yet, after World War II, it was still possible to take trolleys or interurbans to such places as Kennywood; Rocky Glen; the parks at Long Beach and Santa Monica, California; Riverview in Chicago; and Cleveland's Euclid Beach. And in a classic case of history repeating itself, Great America in Santa Clara, California, a relatively new theme park dating from 1976, is now served by San Jose's new "light rail" (the politically correct word for "trolley") line!

Copycats

While it is usually easier to copy an idea than to come up with something original, it is doubtful that Cincinnati's Coney Island set out to copy the New York original. Although it was located on a river, it could in no way be construed as an island. In fact, the name of the park was Ohio Grove. "The Coney Island of the West" was merely a subtitle used in an attempt to capitalize on

LUNA PARK, PITTSBURGH, PA.   8069

the rising popularity and notoriety of the original. The Venice, California, amusement area was also known as the "Coney Island of the Pacific," and Summit Beach Park was known as the "Coney Island of Akron," but Ohio Grove was the only American park known to have actually adopted the Coney name as its own.

Luna Park, Cleveland

Cleveland's Luna Park perhaps came closest to recreating the splendor of the New York prototype. In the top left illustration, note again the recurring moon theme. In the above scene, countless electric lights provide an enchanting ambiance at Cleveland's park, just like at Coney's Luna. BOTH, AUTHOR'S COLLECTION

Luna Park, Pittsburgh

Shoot-the-Chutes were signature rides at Luna and White City parks. A Chute boat is being hoisted up the lift hill at Pittsburgh's Luna Park circa 1908. A few of these classic rides would survive well into the twentieth century, such as at Chicago's Riverview Park, and the late 1990s, Pittsburgh's Kennywood Park recreated a Shoot-the-Chutes in its new Lost Kennywood section. AUTHOR'S COLLECTION

By far the most copied name in amusement park history was Luna Park. Just two years after the opening of the original, Frederick Ingersoll was opening the first two of his masterful copies. His Pittsburgh and Cleveland Luna Parks both opened in 1906 and although simpler in design than the original, were still very close in look and feel. Each succeeding Luna Park emulated the New York prototype while incorporating some of its own unique character. At last count, there had been some 60 Luna Park copies worldwide. Eventually, the magic of Luna wore off, and by the beginning of the Great Depression, virtually all the North American Luna Parks were either gone or had changed their names.

Coney's Dreamland spawned a few namesakes, too. Rochester, New York, had a Dreamland, and there was a Dreamland-On-The-Bay near Baltimore, Maryland. Both are long gone. Nowadays the name is used in some other countries, but Dreamland in Nara, Japan, is really a 1960s copy of the original Disneyland

Incandescent lighting was still a novelty at the turn of the century, and the rest of the country followed Coney's lead in using it to enhance park grounds. The most obvious were parks named Electric Park. It is unknown which was first, but Electric Park in Kansas City, Missouri, was the largest and best known. Others appeared in Kankakee, Illinois; Joplin, Missouri; Baltimore; Detroit, Michigan; Kinderhook (Albany), New York; plus Galveston and San Antonio, Texas.

There have been a few individual copies of famous parks. Coney's Steeplechase had such unrelated siblings as Steeplechase Pier in Atlantic City and Steeplechase Island in Bridgeport, Connecticut, and the original name of Paragon Park on Nastasket Beach at Hull, Massachusetts, was Steeplechase.

The 1893 Columbian Exposition in Chicago gave birth to a nearby amusement park shortly after the fair closed. In a strange twist, the park took its name, not from the midway, but from the Exposition's less popular White City section. Modeling the layout and majestic architecture of the fair, the central lagoon featured a large *Shoot-the-Chutes*, patterned after Coney's Luna.

White City was second only to Luna Park as a popular name, and White Cities soon appeared in New Haven, Savin Rock and Westhaven, Connecticut; Atlanta, Georgia; Louisville, Kentucky; Worcester, Massachusetts; Springfield, Missouri; Binghamton and Syracuse, New York; Cleveland and Dayton, Ohio; Philadelphia, Pennsylvania; Bellingham and Seattle, Washington; as well as Oshkosh and Sheboygan, Wisconsin.

White City survivor, Denver

The Mile-High City boasted a particularly large, elaborate White City that in part still stands—it's today's wonderful Lakeside Park. Although nearly all the rides and attractions visible in this panoramic scene from circa 1910 have been replaced with newer amusements, the landmark tower (readily visible from nearby Interstate 70), the miniature railroad circling what is now Lake Rhoda, and the railroad's depot (at right along the lake in the scene below) remain in operation. AUTHOR'S COLLECTION

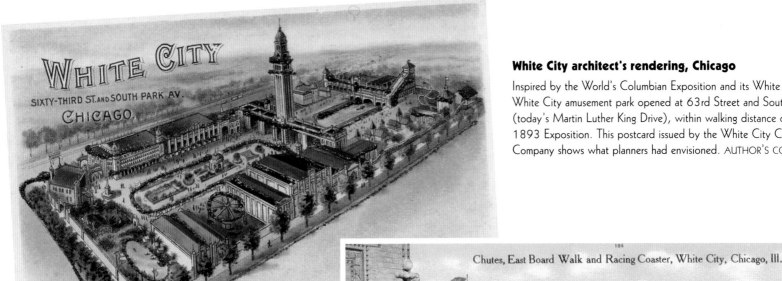

WHITE CITY, DENVER, COLO.

White City architect's rendering, Chicago

Inspired by the World's Columbian Exposition and its White City section, White City amusement park opened at 63rd Street and South Park Avenue (today's Martin Luther King Drive), within walking distance of the site of the 1893 Exposition. This postcard issued by the White City Construction Company shows what planners had envisioned. AUTHOR'S COLLECTION

Chutes, East Board Walk and Racing Coaster, White City, Chicago, Ill.

The thing that set the original Luna Park apart from subsequent imitators was that owner-operators Thompson and Dundy were showmen. The ratio of spectacular shows to rides was very high. The imitators were successful only at copying the name or the overall theme. Staging live spectacles required huge investments of money, large crowds, and a reliable finger on the pulse of the public—to know when to update the show. Besides, everyone knows that a copy is not as sharp as the original. Ultimately, the spreading amusement parks, while throwing in the occasional live show or circus act, concentrated instead on giving the park patrons thrilling rides, engaging games, and a place to eat and relax. In retrospect, it turned out to be a formula with longevity.

Finally, the very things that made the early copycats popular were to be their downfall. The parks that relied heavily on the ride/show extravaganzas had trouble competing with the motion picture. Electricity quickly became commonplace, and the racially troubled times later in the twentieth century would not be the time to have a park called White City. In the end, it is only those parks that have been able to adapt to the changing times, that have survived.

White City as built

Located on Chicago's South Side, White City served as a popular amusement venue for many years until Riverview emerged as Chicago's premier park. This pre-World War I view of White City reveals the Racing Coaster, the Devil's Gorge (note the huge bat decoration), a portion of the Chutes, carousel (in building next to Devil's Gorge), and boardwalk. AUTHOR'S COLLECTION

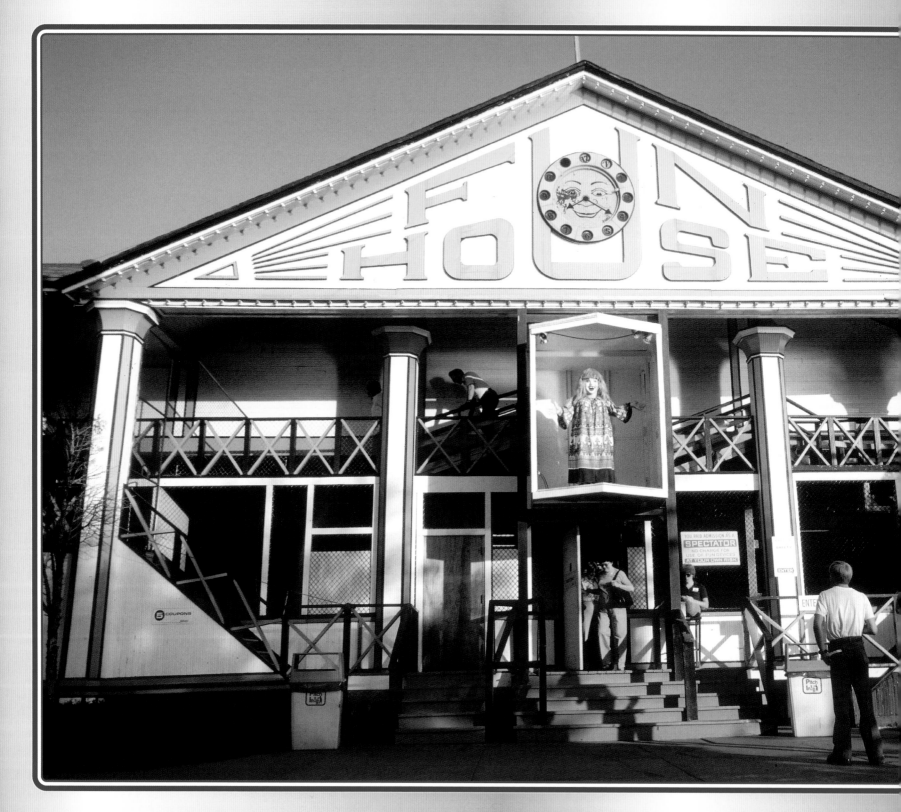

Fun House, Lakeside Park, Denver

Well into the 1980s, Denver's Lakeside Park was home to a classic vintage fun house, complete with moving floors, mazes, slides, and a human roulette wheel. Fun houses were a staple of the many attractions of an amusement park's midway. MIKE SCHAFER

Neon Snoopy, Buckroe Beach, Hampton, Virginia

FACING PAGE: Neon lighting provided essential midway mood after the sun set. This bit of Snoopy neon art "flew" across the top of a concession stand at the now-defunct Buckroe Beach Amusement Park on the Virginia Coast. OTTO P. DOBNICK

HURRY, HURRY
Step Right Up, Folks!

The midway, an amusement park's artery of fun and food

The smell of cotton candy permeates the air. Lead projectiles fell iron targets, hard leather orbs shatter earthen dinnerware, and barkers' "come-ons" penetrate the rumbling of wheels and the blare of band instruments to create a cacophony that is uniquely the midway. Corn dogs, French fries, and ice cream taste better here than anywhere else on the planet.

Funk & Wagnalls defines a midway as "The space, at a fair or exposition, assigned for the display of exhibits and along which the various amusements are situated." In amusement park context, the term began as the "Midway

Midway entrance, Playland Park

Handsome Art Deco structurework at Playland in Rye, New York, helps organize park components. This gateway to Playland's Midway stands between the Dragon Coaster and the site of the erstwhile Aeroplane Coaster. MIKE SCHAFER

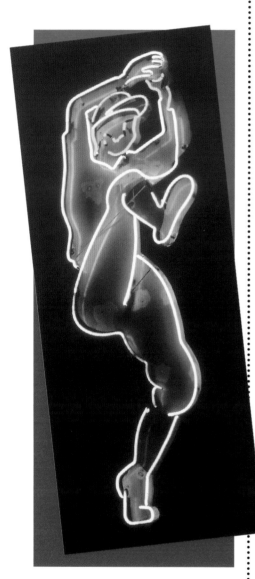

Neon Art

The timeless, dazzling quality of neon makes it a staple of midway lighting. This pitcher is one of countless decorative touches at fabulous Kennywood Park near Pittsburgh. OTTO P. DOBNICK

Plaisance" at the Columbian Exposition, Chicago's 1893 World's Fair. Although aliases include The Pike, Zone, Bowery, Pan, Warpath, Pay Streak, and Gay Way, if the smell of cotton candy is in the air, a midway by any other name will still smell as sweet. Going back to the world's fairs and expositions that pioneered the route of amusement park development, the midway referred to the entire amusement area as a way of distinguishing rides and other base amusements from the more enlightening and uplifting portion of an exposition. But as the amusement park evolved as a species all its own, the midway became more than just an avenue linking attractions.

Amusement park midways consist of side shows, penny arcades, games, souvenir kiosks, fun houses, small rides, and food stands. As the park's main artery, the midway brings life and energy to the amusement park.

Sideshow saga

Once upon a time, the sideshow, with its Bearded Lady, Tattooed Man, and the Dog-Faced Boy, ruled the midway, at least in the large parks. When amusement parks and circuses were in earlier stages of development, the general population was perhaps more insensitive to broad differences in physical appearance. At a time when codes of dress and behavior were more strictly observed, the only place many true oddities of nature could find a way to make a reasonable living was in a sideshow. In the age of "political correctness" and high-tech modern medicine, extreme human oddities are increasingly hard to find, and parading someone's misfortune or uniqueness in front of a crowd for personal gain is simply unacceptable. Chicago's Riverview Park at one time boasted the largest aggregation of strange-looking human beings in North America, but, with so many competing side shows, Coney Island had it beat by a mile.

Samuel W. Gumpertz, a Missouri showman instrumental in the construction of Coney Island's Dreamland, brought 300 midgets from world's fairs and circuses across America to his experimental miniature community. The success of Lilliputia, as Gumpertz's exhibition was titled, encouraged him to expand his venture in exhibitionism. His international travels resulted in the transport of the most unusual and grotesque of human beings. He brought a tribe of 212 Bantocs (Spanish speaking Filipinos) through immigration in 1905 to please his crowds with their poison dart expertise. He also brought in 18 fierce, bearded Algerian horsemen and 19 wild men from Borneo. In Burma he found women who had stretched their necks 14 inches by wearing an increasing number of brass rings around them. Another dozen women with lips extended around wooden platters up to 10 inches wide were put on display from French Equatorial Africa.

When Dreamland closed, Gumpertz devoted himself to the exhibition of strange people, and he had little difficulty convincing them to join his operation. After all, they were more at home in the low-paying steady jobs that offered them a sense of community, living at Coney Island among their peers. The usual included Captain Copp, the human tattoo gallery; Ursa the bear girl; 615 pounds of Baby Alpine; two men who stood over eight feet tall; Lionel, the dog-faced boy; Princess Wee Wee, just 34 inches high; Rob Roy, albino wonder; and Schrief Afendl, the human salamander. Most freak shows today are circus or carnival operations and are more likely to feature non-human quirks of the animal kingdom, such as two-headed cows.

Insert coin here

It's hard to find anything for a penny anymore, although everyone still wants to throw in their two cents. The so-called penny arcade has become a misnomer, more often than not being literally a two-bit operation. Today's arcade games take quarters or 25-cent tokens, with some games requiring several per player, but there was a time when most all coin-operated attractions could be enjoyed for a penny per play. Until just a few years ago, penny-operated machines could still be found at some traditional amusement parks. However, these machines have increased in value as collectibles, and the risk of damage has become too high to allow them to be played by the public.

The first coin-operated machines were used for vending. A coin-operated vending machine was described by Heron of Alexandria around 200 B.C., predating the penny arcade and the amusement park by about 2,000 years. This machine, discovered in Egypt, was a simple device dispensing holy water when a coin was dropped in, pushing down a lever that operated a valve. But not until electricity, improved tools, and patrons with "spare coin," in the late 1800s, did the development of intricate mechanical devices rapidly advance. In 1871 a patent was granted for "The Race Course Bank" in which two tin horses revolved atop a cast-iron base when a nickel was inserted and a string was pulled. Although designed as a bank, the toy soon found its way into saloons, where "players" would speculate rather than save, by betting on the horses. Inadvertently, the gambling machine and the arcade game had been invented.

Originally, all coin-operated machines were called "coin-in-the-slot" machines. Shortened to "slot" machines, the name eventually was applied exclusively to gambling devices, and amusement devices became known as "coin-ops." By 1891, gambling machines were enticing

Arcade, Castles & Coasters, Phoenix, Arizona

The arcade at Phoenix's Castles & Coasters park in 1995 was a dazzling cornucopia of pinball machines and video games.

Game row at Crystal Beach, Ontario

Business appears to be a bit slow at the gaming booths at Crystal Beach in 1983. The center booth features the "Hoopla" game in which hoops are tossed at prizes.
OTTO P. DOBNICK

patrons to "take a chance" in cities all over the country, while Edison's phonographs came with coin slots and were being set up in special parlors to generate revenue. As those became successful, other devices including stereoscopic viewers, strength testers, fortune tellers, and the Kinescope (an early television-related device, another Edison invention) were added to create the penny arcade. Elaborate arcades populated not only amusement parks, but the main streets of America. By the end of World War I, they were relegated to amusement parks, but the Depression brought the return of the stand-alone arcade as well as the pinball machine.

Gaffers play hanky-panky

Derived from the derogatory term "hanky-panky," the hanky-pank harkens to a time when the carneys ruled the midway, and trickery and sleight-of-hand ruled the games. Although hanky-pank and other nicknames—"flat games," "hat man," "quay boss"—have all but disappeared

from usage, almost any career park person still recognizes them as the once universally known terms of the trade designating certain (and sometimes shady) midway activities, a holdover from the days when carneys ran the midway and "gaffing" (cheating or fixing) of games was common. The quay boss tried to keep everything under control, usually cracking down on the dishonesty only when there were complaints. It's no surprise then, that William F. Mangels is quoted as once saying, "No American amusement park which permits and fosters games of chance can escape public scorn." But that was at a time when games competed with rides for the patron's dollar (or nickel, as the case may have been). Historically, park-goers spent more money on the games than on the rides—and Mangels was first and foremost a ride manufacturer. To him, games were competition.

In those days, the games generally were concessions, with each concessionaire competing for patrons and profits. The games were referred to as "games of chance," with chance being the operative word. The game player had little chance of beating the odds in the first place, and if the game was rigged, almost no chance. Gaffing a wheel-of-fortune, for example, could be accomplished simply by using a concealed foot pedal to put tension on a string around the axle. An experienced operator could stop the wheel at will on any number.

Contrary to what one might think, the primary purpose of gaffing amusement park games was not just to cheat the customer but also to allow a shill to win. Nobody would play a game very long if the house did all the winning, and an operator apparently losing his shirt would attract large crowds pressing to get in on the action. A planted "winner" periodically took his prizes around to the back of the booth and changed hats to come back and win some more. Most hat men were clean-cut college students on their summer vacations, and they usually worked as roving ambassadors for a number of games in the park.

Occasionally, the operator, by gaffing, would allow a real player to win, as it was in the concessionaire's best interest that there be *some* winners. Although in the early part of the century it was not uncommon for

games to be played for money, today's games of chance involve only prizes—preferably big enough to be seen by all as the winners carry them around the park. The words "Win one of those for me!" are still powerful on the midway.

At one time, games using real dice were popular on the midway. The use of weighted and shaved dice was fairly common, however, and in the interest of proper appearances most of these games disappeared long ago. Games that have even the appearance of gambling have generally been eschewed by reputable operators, with the exception of bingo (or, as some parks call it, lotto or even keno). If bingo games are okay for churches to operate, what's so heinous about a bingo parlor at an amusement park? Besides, bingo was the most difficult game to gaff. Bingo never really made the transition to theme parks, but it can still be found in some traditional parks.

More games people play

The most popular games among the youngest gamblers in the park are not really gambles at all. Referred to as "Everytimes," games like Grab Bag and the Fish Tank award every

Cutout cutups

Long a staple of traditional parks, gag props with cutout openings that folks could stick their mugs through were simple but effective entertainment. Park enthusiasts Elaine Hooley and Mike Danshaw ham it up in a fake roller coaster prop at Kennywood Park in 1980.
MIKE SCHAFER

Mirror mayhem

It wouldn't be a real amusement park without distorted mirrors to change your outlook on life—or what you look like in real life. Maureene Gulbrandsen and son Donny guffaw at one mirror's interpretation of mother and son at Elitch Gardens, Denver.
MIKE SCHAFER

player a prize, every time. As the patron of the Fish Tank triumphantly hooks a fake fish (or in the dry versions, a roly-poly duck or clown), he or she most often finds a number "1" on the bottom, which entitles the winner to any prize . . . on the first shelf only. Of course, the numbers for the higher shelves—and better prizes—are considerably more scarce.

Shooting galleries have always been a hit on the midway. The most popular were cork galleries, where cork-gun-wielding patrons could shoot down celluloid dolls they then claimed as prizes. Ping-pong rifles, shooting at cards, and suction-cup archery were among the other types, but most all of these have disappeared. Balloon darts was another game that was a lot of fun even if the prizes seldom amounted to much. Popping an inflated balloon by throwing darts at it was satisfying enough for most customers, but it was always harder than it looked. About the only place one can find balloon darts nowadays is at a traveling carnival.

One of the most heavily patronized gallery games anywhere was the Mow-'Em-Down machine-gun gallery. The patron got 100 shots at a paper target with an authentic-looking, air-operated tommy gun. If the player could shoot the star on the target completely out, including all points of the star, he won.

For decades, the best shooting galleries had BB rifles connected to an air compressor. The BB shot was steel, so that it would not be malformed when striking the target (iron ducks, jumping rabbits, gong-centered bull's eyes, and the like) or the backdrop, thereby allowing it to be reused constantly. Alas, while some still exist, most of the games featuring projectiles that can do real damage are being retired, and shooting galleries that used regulation .22 rifles and real ammunition are a thing of the past. What concessionaire would want to keep something around that could be used for a holdup?

The games that have lasting power are the games of skill, such as throwing baseballs at something that can be knocked over for a prize. The milk bottle pitch has changed through the years—for one thing, the "bottles" used to be made of iron—but has never wavered in popularity. Using a baseball, the player must knock three aluminum milk bottles, set up pyramid-style, off their platform, with three pitches. It sounds easy, and it *is* easy to knock them down, but all three bottles have to be knocked completely off the platform to win a prize—and *that's* not so easy.

The Cat Pitch is another deceptively easy-looking favorite using baseballs. The patron can win in three pitches merely by tipping over three of the dozens of fluffy cats apparently standing shoulder to shoulder on racks about 12 feet away. It looks like the cat's meow, but the solid bodies on the cats comprise less than a third of their total apparent width, most of which is light fluff standing straight out from the sides. Most hurled baseballs pass right through the airy fluff in-between. Even when you know how difficult it is, the fact that it looks easy, combined with the conviction that "certainly this time I can hit all three . . ." keeps patrons coming back again and again.

Today, most parks prefer tossing games to the more violent hurling games. The Block Pitch is an old toss game that still enjoys popularity. The hoops tossed in a block pitch range in size from about three inches to the size of a

hula hoop in diameter, depending on the size of the prize. But, merely ringing the prize does not a winner make; the hoop must settle flat to the table around the block on which the prize stands.

Another variation of the toss game that remains popular today uses coins rather than rings. When electricity was still a novelty, the Electric Pitch involved a flat board almost completely covered with electric contact points, at which the patron tossed a coin in the hopes of touching two or more contacts as it came to rest, and thereby creating an electric circuit that lit up lights or set off bells. Nowadays, coins are tossed in an attempt to get them to stay in a shallow dish.

In the Basket Pitch, the patron attempts to toss a softball into what looks like an ordinary bushel basket, in the hopes that the baseball will stay inside. However, because the special five-ounce ball easily bounces out of the taut bottom of the baskets, only those who toss the ball in a low arc at the side of the tilted basket have any hope of winning. An updated version of this game that has enjoyed immense popularity of late is the Basketball Pitch. The trick here is that nothing about the equipment—height, distance, size of the hoop, and even the size of the ball—is regulation, and the basketball itself is pumped up so hard that it tends to bounce wildly.

Among the games of skill that have disappeared at amusement parks is the dunk-tank. A "bozo" sat perched on a board over a tub of water, and his job was to hurl insults at patrons, enticing them to pay to hurl baseballs at a six-inch target that would trigger the board and dump the bozo into the water. A bozo really good at his job could so enrage customers that they would start throwing the baseballs directly at him, instead of at the target, and for that reason the bozo always sat behind a protective screen.

Television's famed Bozo the Clown supposedly got his name from this game.

The Hi-Striker is an amusement park/carnival classic. The patron rolls up his sleeves and takes a wild swing with a huge mallet at a catapult board in an often futile attempt to launch a weight to the top of a high column and ring the bell. In the old days, the operator could keep the carrying wire so slack that even Paul Bunyan couldn't ring the bell, but these days the parks want all the over-testosteroned showoffs to look good for their girlfriends—and therefore spend more money. This age-old game is a classic that almost never fails to draw a crowd.

Today's guess-your-weight (or age) game is a sure revenue-generator, as you must pay for the privilege of being the subject of a guess. If you lose, you're out a buck or so, but even if you "win," the prize you'll receive will undoubtedly cost the park but a fraction of what you paid to "win." In effect, the operator has simply sold you an object at great mark up. If nothing else, it's great fun for those who don't look their age or weight.

Skee Ball, once a product of the Philadelphia Toboggan Company—longtime builder of coasters, carousels, and other amusement devices—remains one of the most popular amusement games ever. In Skee Ball, patrons "bowl" heavy, softball-size wooden balls (usually nine per play) down a narrow alley toward ramped-up concentric, circular targets—the smallest netting the biggest points. As players rack up points, the Skee Ball machine spits out coupons (usually emblazoned with the park's name), redeemable at the prize counter. The perennially popular sport has such a following that some parks, including new theme parks, have entire buildings lined with Skee Ball alleys.

Among the new wave of games that coincide with the theme-park era are games like Boom

NO CHARGE IF I FAIL TO GUESS YOUR WEIGHT WITHIN THREE POUNDS

FINDING HER WEIGH

The weight-guessing game

At an unidentified amusement location circa 1900, this carney exhibits an interesting method of determining a person's weight that today would bring sexual-harassment lawsuits. Nonetheless, the expression on the woman's face says it all. AUTHOR'S COLLECTION

Skee Ball, Crystal Beach

(FACING PAGE) Randy Rasmussen of Eureka, California, tries his hand at Skee Ball at Crystal Beach, Ontario, in 1984. Miles of tickets spewed out by automatic Skee-Ball machines are hoarded by players until it's time to redeem them for the prize of choice at the park's prize counter. MIKE SCHAFER

Ball, where a row of patrons shoot rubber balls from a cannon at Skee Ball-type targets. Another popular shooting game is the Balloon Race wherein multiple players shoot a stream of water into a clown's mouth to inflate a balloon. The player to pop their balloon first, wins. Variations of this game have horses or cars that race. Shooting a steady stream of water at your target continuously causes your race "vehicle" to go faster.

"Gypsy" operations

Some of the most popular midway attractions are those that have historically been referred to as "gypsy" operations. Shear joints, where artists cut out the patron's silhouette from a piece of paper, caricature artists, and fortune tellers are all attractions that are extremely portable. Often these operations are set up in different locations on the midway, based on shifting traffic patterns. Photo studios, jewelry engravers, T-shirt and coffee mug stencilers, and hat monogrammers are similar gypsy operations that are often transitory between parks. Sometimes these attractions are operated by the park, but historically they have been concessionaires that will set up at a park for a season and move to another the next.

A fading favorite: the fun house

Although the fun house was not usually a concession, it wasn't considered a ride, either. The classic fun house features a collection of attractions, usually in one big building, where patrons were welcome to stay and amuse themselves for as long as they liked. Although every amusement park had a fun house, without question, the largest and most famous of all was the Pavilion of Fun in Steeplechase Park at Coney Island, New York. Covering several acres, it was the be all and end all of fun houses. In fact, Steeplechase's owner, George Tilyou, is credited with inventing many of the stunts found in fun houses.

There were no rules as to what constituted a fun house, but most had similar stunts. Slides, with literal and figurative twists and turns, were among the most popular house attractions. Most fun houses had a mirror maze in which the customers invariably got lost. As far as mirrors go, no fun house, anywhere, was complete without its distorting mirrors.

Just walking through a fun house usually had its ups and downs. Walking through the rolling barrel was a task too difficult for many patrons,

Artists on the midway

Young artists sketch out caricatures for folks strolling the midway at Kennywood Park near Pittsburgh on a balmy summer evening in 1980; in the background is Le Cachot, a dark ride. An outgrowth of what has sometimes been referred to as "gypsy" operations, today's "gypsies" are often talented students working their way through college. MIKE SCHAFER

The Fun House, Lakeside Park

Giggling youngsters whirl away on the human roulette wheel in the venerable old Fun House at Lakeside Park in Denver, Colorado, in 1983. Other attractions in this, the main room of the building, included a walk-through barrel and slides. MIKE SCHAFER

Fun house barrel roll

The walk-through rotating barrel was and remains the archetypical funhouse stunt. This scene from early in the twentieth century shows the "Barrel of Fun" (and a bit of leg of one momentarily incapacitated patron) at Revere Beach near Boston, Massachusetts. AUTHOR'S COLLECTION

so often alongside there was an alternative walk-way—but even it had some tomfoolery to it, such as a moving floor. Other weird walkways included one with wall-to-wall discs in the floor, rotating in opposite directions. Some funhouse stairways, split down the middle, oscillated in such a fashion that the right side would slide up a step while the left side slid down, and so on in rapid succession. The camelback walkway heaved up and down.

The human roulette wheel was another funhouse entertainment for people who wanted to see how long they could resist centrifugal force. Patrons piled themselves at the center of a large floor-level wheel. As speed built up in the disc on which they sat, bodies would be spun off onto the floor. The winner (usually the one who sat dead-center on the disc) often got so dizzy that they, too, were ultimately flung off into the side wall. Back in the days when girls still wore skirts to amusement parks, the human roulette wheel was one of the most popular people-watching spots in the park. In fact, fun houses were as much a spectator sport, as a participatory one. Boys used to hang around for hours outside *Aladdin's Castle* at Riverview Park in Chicago, just to watch the girls who didn't know enough to hold their skirts down as they walked over hidden air jets on an outside walkway.

A "walk-through" is related to the fun house in that it is housed in a building and patrons are on their own to move through. The difference is that the pathway is much more structured, with patrons following a specific route and kept moving. The most common theme of a walk-through is that of a haunted house or castle, with a darkened labyrinth of a walkway as its centerpiece. Patrons walk past exhibits or animated displays (opening coffins, skeletons rattling in dungeon chains, and so forth) and through special rooms that feature a number of optional doors—most leading to nowhere or simply to another door in the room—which explorers must navigate to find the correct one that will allow them to continue through the rest of the attraction. Although walk-throughs are becoming less common as parks switch to ride-through dark rides which provide more control over customers, a few classic walk-throughs are still in operation, such as the *Haunted Castle* at Indiana Beach, Monticello, Indiana. This complex walk-through is on several levels, takes almost 15 minutes to navigate, features numerous spooky displays, and includes one of the most startling tricks ever,

involving an open balcony. We wouldn't dare reveal the results.

The most difficult of all walk-throughs to navigate is the Mystery Shack, where entire rooms tilt but with the furniture and fixtures remaining parallel with the walls. Known by many other names, the Mystery Shack often serves as a stand-alone tourist attraction but it can also be found as part of a larger walk-through. Regardless of name or location, stand in what you think is an upright posture in a Mystery Shack and you'll fall over.

Although you'll still find fun houses in today's traditional amusement parks, they are fun houses

Tipsy House, Dickenson County Amusement Park

Cleverly intertwined with the roller coaster station, the Tipsy House at this well-known amusement park at Arnolds Park, Iowa, is a walk-through attraction with bizarre perspectives and tilted floors, certain to disorient first-timers. OTTO P. DOBNICK

in name only. Usually consisting of mirror mazes and a few innocuous stunts, they contain little that will permit actual injury. Today's litigious society has killed the true, traditional fun houses, and a fatal fire in a walk-through at a New Jersey theme park in the mid-1980s caused the removal of many then-remaining walk-throughs elsewhere.

Let's play a round at the park

Of all the participatory attractions, the most engaging and enduring is that diminutive form of golf known as miniature. Known by such names as Pee Wee, Putt-Putt, and Tom Thumb Golf, miniature golf took America by storm in the 1920s, and then just as quickly all but disappeared in the

House of mirrors

Mirror mazes were usually an integral part of a classic fun house, but oftentimes they served as a stand-alone attraction, as with the Labyrinth Crystal Palace at Denver's Lakeside Park in 1983. MIKE SCHAFER

Miracle Strip, Panama City, Florida

Haunted theming seems to be the most common—and popular—of that applied to participatory visual attractions at parks, be they walk-throughs or dark rides. Miracle Strip at Panama City, Florida, features an elaborate haunted house, as shown in 1987. The park's Skyliner roller coaster is in the background while a gigantic devil head provides relief from real heat while inside, riders enjoy a cool respite on a spinning ride. OTTO P. DOBNICK

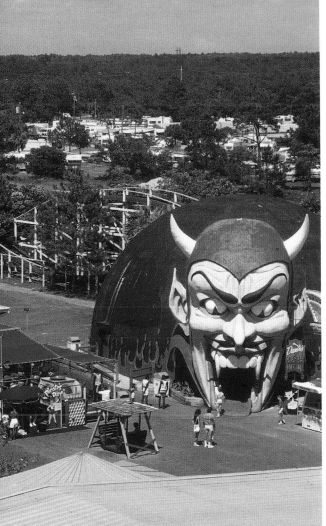

1930s. If not for its presence as an attraction within some amusement parks, it just might have disappeared entirely.

Scaling down the game of golf had already taken the form of such things as putting greens when, in 1916, James Barber hired Edward H. Wiswell to create a small course on the grounds of his estate in Pinehurst, North Carolina. This garden-turned-golf-course, named Thistle Dhu, was not only the first midget golf course to contain all the pleasurable elements of the real game, but may have also been the reason early miniature golf was referred to as garden golf. Made of natural grass, the course was literally carved out of a formal garden. According to legend, upon completion, Mr. Barber looked out over his creation and remarked, "This'll do!" The name stuck, but if it weren't for an article in 1920 in *Country Life* magazine, the world may never have known about his private playground.

Thomas Fairbairn is the next player in this Lilliputian golf story. An Englishman who owned a cotton plantation in Mexico, Fairbairn was obsessed with trying to build a tiny golf course. However, nothing he tried in the way of "greens" would allow him to recreate the colorful hills of his homeland in the arid climate of his Mexican estate. One day Fairbairn noticed that the cotton-seed hulls on the floor near the cotton gin had become trampled by the workers into a smooth surface. Experimentation began immediately.

The ultimate miniature golf course

Miniature golf has been a common attraction in park midways for many years, and they can still be found at a number of traditional amusement parks. Miniature golf has experienced a boom in recent years, and in some cases it's become the tail wagging the dog. Golf 'n' Stuff in Norwalk, California, is principally a super miniature golf course with amusement rides and an arcade on the side.

Food on the midway, Idora Park

Good old American pop-culture food (never mind the calories and carbs) is as much an amusement park ritual as a carousel ride. Summer evening breezes stir the leafy canopy over the midway at Youngstown, Ohio's, Idora Park in 1983 as customers line up for games and food. MIKE SCHAFER

Grinding the fuzzy hulls, adding oil to bind them together, dying the concoction green, and rolling it over sand gave him the surface he had been looking for. Fairbairn patented the processed material and in 1925 founded Miniature Golf Courses of America, Inc.

The following year, two New Yorkers, Drake Delanoy and John Ledbetter, built what is reported to be the city's first outdoor miniature golf course, on the roof of a skyscraper. After trying a variety of putting surfaces, they claimed to have stumbled upon the cottonseed-hull surface, overlooking the fact that there probably wasn't a single cottonseed hull to be found in all of New York City. Fairbairn's Miniature Golf Courses of America nailed them for patent infringement, but in 1928 the two entities came to a royalties agreement. Delanoy and Ledbetter went on to open 150 mini-golf courses on New York City rooftops.

Meanwhile, down south, high atop Lookout Mountain, Georgia, the game of miniature golf as we know it was being invented. The story begins

in 1924 when Garnet and Frieda Carter became owners of ten acres of land in a parcel of 600 acres being developed into the community of Fairyland by Carter and a business associate. Fairyland Inn and a full-sized golf course were built to be the centerpiece of the community. The true details of what happened next seem to be lost. One source claims that Fairyland's 1926 Tom Thumb Golf was the ingenious invention of Garnet Carter to entertain his guests at the inn. Other accounts claim either that Garnet built the course to occupy regular golfers while the big course was being completed or to entertain the children of his guests. Two other stories have Frieda as the designer of the course, possibly as a way to entertain golf widows whose husbands were out playing real golf. One of these stories is certainly possible, as Frieda was the designer of the Rock City Gardens that became known worldwide, as well as many of its buildings.

Whatever the origin, there was something unusual about the course that made it different from its predecessors. Previous designs had concentrated on the scaling down of the real golf experience into a garden-sized course, complete with natural grass. Although Carter's course did indeed feature natural grass, he added pieces of tile, sewer pipe, hollow logs, and other obstacles as well as fairyland statues as decoration, and the little links took on a new twist.

The small course on the front lawn of the Fairyland Inn became a major draw. Carter quickly cut a deal with Fairbairn for licensing of the cottonseed-hull playing surface and in 1929 patented his obstacle course under the name Tom Thumb Golf—just in time for the mini-golf fad to catch on. By 1930, over 3,000 Tom Thumb Golf franchises had been sold. Conneaut Lake Park and Kennywood Park, in western Pennsylvania, are just two of many amusement parks that installed Tom Thumb Golf in 1930. By this time, many competing companies were also offering their own version of pygmy golf.

The 1920s were a time of tremendous social change and outrageous fads. Miniature golf just happened to be the last of these wacky crazes. However, the trend ended as quickly as it started. By the summer of 1931, market saturation, the deepening Depression, and legal restrictions had all but killed the game. Only within amusement parks, where it was a relaxing break from the thrill rides, did the game continue to thrive.

In the 1950s, new entrepreneurs arrived on the miniature golf scene, ushering in a new era of growth in the early 1960s. Coinciding with the explosion of suburbia, these courses provided a close-by form of entertainment at a time when the traditional amusement park— by this time often located in a decaying part of town—was rapidly disappearing. The continuing growth of the suburbs crowded out most of these courses, but a few survived, grew, and morphed into an entirely new type of park of their own (Chapter 9).

Lettuce entertain you

Fresh air, exercise, thrills, chills, and dares conjure up an appetite in almost every parkgoer. And some people relish parks for the food alone. "Grab joints" have provided inexpensive and fast fare to thrill-seekers throughout amusement park history. Aside from hamburgers, cold beer, lemonade, and soda pop, parks across the country have contributed to the establishment of a cuisine seldom seen in the company of anything other than a midway or wild, heart-stopping rides.

Like most of the trappings of today's amusement culture, food trends began on Coney Island. In 1867 Charles Feltman owned a pie-wagon that delivered his freshly baked pies to the inns and lager-beer saloons that lined Coney's beaches. His clients also wanted hot sandwiches to serve to their customers, but his wagon was small, and he knew that it would be hard to manage making a variety of sandwiches in a confined space. He thought that perhaps something simple like a hot sausage served on a roll might be the solution. He presented his problem to a wheelwright in

Food stand, Mountain Park, Holyoke, Massachusetts

Good things come from little concession stands. This brightly lit concession stand at the now-defunct Mountain Park near Holyoke in 1983 offered an appealing variety of fare, including frozen bananas. MIKE SCHAFER

Brooklyn named Donovan who had built his pie-wagon. The man saw no problem in building a tin-lined chest to keep the rolls fresh and rigging a small charcoal stove inside to boil sausages. When the wheelwright finished the installation, they fired up the stove for a test run. Donovan thought that the sausage sandwich was a strange idea as Feltman boiled the succulent pork sausage and placed it between a roll. The wheelwright tasted it and liked it. The hot dog was born.

The hot dog, however, didn't go unchallenged. Rumors abounded that the sausages were made of dog meat, and the politicians alleged that they found a rendering plant making sausages out of dead horses for Coney Island establishments. John McKane protested that, "Nobody knows what is inside these sausages." He slapped an excise tax of $200 on every sausage stand. "We can not dictate to a man what he must sell," said the chief, "but we can make it hard for him to carry on his business."

Fortunately for Feltman and others, the rumors soon subsided and the food became popular again. Feltman's all-time record was serving 100,000 people and 40,000 hot dogs in a single day. Feltman had seven huge grills scattered about its premises, each grilling hot dogs by the thousands. And by 1921, when the extension of the subway brought millions more to the beach, Feltman's served more than 3.5 million customers; in 1922 more

Concession stand, Knoebels Grove, Elysburg, Pennsylvania

Neon lighting can make what would be an ordinary grab joint into a work of art where you can buy your favorite park food. The Kandy Korner is at Knoebels Grove amusement park in east central Pennsylvania in 1985. MIKE SCHAFER

than 4 million customers and in 1923 nearly five and a quarter million customers. The majority, by then, bought hot dogs for ten cents each.

Another venerable institution on the Bowery was Stauch's. It differed from most of the other beach establishments since it was solidly built of brick and stone like it belonged in urban Manhattan. Inside it was comfortable and roomy and attracted an upper-class clientele to its dining room and dance hall.

In 1877, Louis Stauch came to Coney Island as a 16-year-old and got a job playing piano in Daniel Welch's saloon. By day he was a dishwasher and potato peeler, and by night he was a waiter, busboy, barkeep, and piano player. It was hard work for $15 a month, but after two years the frugal teenager had saved $310—enough to lease Welch's place for $700 a year. He did so well that he signed a ten-year lease at $2,000 a year. When a storm wrecked the restaurant, he built a new one. Stauch was a hard worker, silent and humorless, but a good-hearted little man. He gained a reputation for serving a good, well-cooked meal at a reasonable price, so his reputation soon spread far and wide.

The Bowery burned several times, but Stauch persistently rebuilt his restaurant. It became an immense building that at the time housed the biggest dance hall in the world. Stauch's was comfortable, more so than usual because its owner lived there. He ate in his restaurant and slept in his restaurant. When he married late in life, he even spent his honeymoon in his restaurant. In a quarter century, he never spent a single night away from Coney despite his friends' attempts to get him out. In fact, one day they shanghaied him by train to Atlantic City and checked him into a hotel. But he managed to sneak away and return to Coney, where he slept in his restaurant, his record intact. When Prohibition came in the early 1920s, Stauch finally sold his beloved establishment.

Nathan Handwerker visited Coney Island in the summer of 1915 and saw a HELP WANTED sign at Feltman's restaurant. Although he was a manager of a modest restaurant in downtown Manhattan, he decided to take the job slicing hot dog rolls for a living. Within a year, Nathan had saved $300 by living on the cheap and eating free hot dogs at Feltman's—it was enough money to rent the ground floor of a building located near the corner of Surf and Stilwell Avenues. He installed counters in the weathered clapboard building and nailed up large red signs proclaiming the five-cent hot dog. But Nathan nearly went broke. Even when he offered root beer on the house and threw in a free pickle, the public was suspicious. They ignored him and took their dimes to Feltman's.

Then in the early 1920s the subway/elevated extension enabled millions of New York's poor to reach Coney Island for only a nickel. Nathan's stand had a strategic position directly between the transit terminal and the boardwalk. But even they, with only nickels in their pockets, were mistrustful of Nathan's cheap price because, in their experience, anything so cheap had to be inferior. To draw business, Nathan resorted to hiring derelicts to sit at his counter and eat free hot

Stauch's, Coney Island, N. Y.

Stauch's, Coney Island

Famous Stauch's restaurant and dance hall at Coney Island was a bastion of civilization in the frenetic surroundings of the Bowery. The building's Beaux Arts style reflected a growing movement that had been inspired by buildings at the 1893 World's Columbian Exposition in Chicago.

Being a pig, sucks

In an effort to inspire people to properly dispose of trash, the folks at Crystal Beach, Ontario, devised a suction-operated trash bin disguised as a pig—Porky the Paper Eater—in a mushroom house. OTTO P. DOBNICK

PORKY
THE PAPER EATER

Fake fire fancily fought

Entertainment takes on many forms at amusement parks. At Chicago's White City park circa 1905, firefighters demonstrate how they'll stop the next great Chicago Fire. AUTHOR'S COLLECTION

speed. The material, resembling combed cotton, is twisted onto a cardboard cone or bagged.

Although ice cream itself had been around for hundreds of years, ice cream cones were created and served at the 1904 World's Fair in St. Louis. Pastrymaker Ernest A. Hamwi was selling wafer-like pastries at a concession stand with sugar and other sweets. When a neighboring ice cream stand ran out of dishes, Hamwi rolled some of his wafers into cornucopias, let them cool, and sold them to the ice cream concessionaire who loaded them up with ice cream. However, an ice cream cone mold patent was issued earlier in the year to Italian immigrant Italo Marchiony who claimed he had been making ice cream cones since 1896. He and other claimants challenged Hamwi's right to call himself the originator of the ice cream cone.

With the sweet always comes the salty, and the combination can result in nonstop snacking that warms the hearts of amusement park concession-aires. In 1954 a boardwalk vendor in Ocean City, New Jersey, offered cotton candy on pretzel rods, attempting an unusual marriage of two tastes and favorite mobile snacks. But little beats the old standby, popcorn—already an accepted snack in the late nineteenth century. In 1891, a new recipe—cooking the corn right in its seasoning-as well as a "refined popper" was developed by Dudley Humphrey, of the Euclid Beach Humphrey family, and they were perhaps the first to transport it by wagon to a traveling carnival making a stop in Cleveland. Popcorn has evermore been an essential part of every park. Euclid Beach Park has been closed since 1969, but you can still get the Humphrey family's famous popcorn balls.

While the products and services of food vendors can vary greatly based on regional traditions and tastes, corn dogs, French fries, "elephant ears" (sugar-covered fried dough in the shape of just that), snow cones, popcorn, and giant pretzels have generally been a part of America's amusement park fare for decades. But what would good food be without something to watch while eating?

Since the days of pleasure gardens, refreshments and entertainment have gone hand-in-hand. In fact the first "amusements" at Coney Island were really the ramshackle saloons and dance halls that dotted the beach. Patrons came to listen to the crooners, while being watered, fed, and sometimes fleeced. This was the beginning for a number of entertainers as well. If, in those early days, you happened into Perry's Glass

dogs, but the crowd saw only bums and avoided the place. Then a friend in the theatrical costume business lent him ten white suits and ten stetho-scopes and he dressed ten freshly shaven bums as doctors. When the public saw his sign, "If doctors eat our hot dogs, you know they're good!" they began patronizing his stand. He became so successful that the police were always trying to clear the mass of customers that blocked the broad sidewalk in front of his stand. Although his counter was only 20 feet long, Nathan's sold an average of 75,000 frankfurters every summer weekend. The record was on Decoration Day 1954 when he sold 55,000 hot dogs in a single day. Naturally his counter became bigger, and Nathan's became a year-round operation. On July 6, 1955, he sold his one hundred millionth dog.

In the second half of the nineteenth century, clams were all the rage on Coney Island. Easy to come by at that seaside locale, fresh and ever-plentiful, they were served everywhere and cheaply. Grilled clams doused in rich butter went for a penny at Lucy Vanderveer's restaurant, and a bowl of clam chowder was offered as a bonus to anyone renting bathing wear for 25 cents at Tilyou's Surf House.

Cotton candy could be a mainstay at zoos, circuses, and carnivals as well as amusement parks if it were anything more than spun sugar. Invented in 1830 by (ironically) a dentist, the colorful fine strands are the result of combining sugar and flavoring in a specially designed machine that spins the combination at a high rate of

Pavilion, you might have been served by a singing waiter who would later become as famous as Irving Berlin. At Carey Walsh's, piano player "Ragtime Jimmie" Durante performed with waiter Izzy Iskowitz, later known as Eddie Cantor.

As America and its amusement parks grew, so did the entertainment. When vaudeville swept the nation, amusement parks built theaters. When dancing was the craze, the ballroom became a feature at every major park in the country. During the Great Depression, dancing to the Big Bands became the activity that kept many parks alive. As America's musical tastes changed, so did the shows that parks put on. In the 1960s, many of the

surviving parks invited famous rock 'n' roll acts to perform on their stages.

Ultimately, entire parks have been designed around entertainment. Most notable was Opryland. When the Grand Old Opry moved out of the Ryman Auditorium in Nashville, it moved into a new facility that was part of a multi-million dollar theme park complex. Although the park included themed traditional rides, it always had an emphasis on shows. Though Opryland is gone, its impact can still be seen, particularly among newer theme parks. Today, park visitors find an amazing array of variety shows, giving them an opportunity to take an occasional break from the rides.

Greek theater, Busch Gardens Williamsburg, Virginia

Outdoor entertainment at Busch Gardens Williamsburg (formerly Busch Gardens Old Country) provides a pleasant break from rides while having a bite to eat. OTTO P. DOBNICK

Carousel, Seabreeze Park, Rochester, New York

Seabreeze's pristine carousel displays the mark of a "true" carousel—all white lights (versus the multi-colored lights of a "merry-go-round")—on a summer's day in 1983. Alas, the park's carousel, Wurlitzer band organ, carousel building, and carousel museum was heavily damaged by fire a few years later. OTTO P. DOBNICK

Tilt-A-Whirl sign, Conneaut Lake Park, Pennsylvani

Against a backdrop of Conneaut Lake Park's Ferris wheel, the Tilt-A-Whirl sign beckons riders to that favorite of "flat" rides built by Minnesota-based Sellner Corporation. MIKE SCHAFER

ROUND AND ROUND
Rides of a Lifetime

Carousels, Ferris wheels, dark rides, miniature trains and other favorites

Amusement parks have always brought together popular pastimes and attractions. Picnicking, public bathing, concerts, dancing, stage shows, circus performances, motion pictures, bowling, and roller skating have been part of amusement parks since their beginnings. All have existed outside the amusement park as well—which is to say that these activities, in and of themselves, have little power to attract patrons specifically to an amusement park. What really brings customers through the gates? It's the rides, silly. *That's* the big reason people love amusement parks.

Carousel horse, Dorney Park, Allentown, Pennsylvania

Frozen in time, ornate carved horses (or other animals) are the essence of the carousel. In a hand-crafted carousel, the figures are individual creations, hand-painted. This colorful steed was photographed in 1978. LEE O. BUSH

Carousel chariot, Dorney Park

For those not inclined to climb up on one of the galloping figures of a carousel, a ride in one of the chariots allowed you to still be part of the fun. This chariot on the Dorney Park carousel was repainted between the 1970 and 1971 season, and the artist—in this instance a Mr. Ed Walters—signed his craftsmanship. LEE O. BUSH

A case could even be made that what defines an entertainment venue as an amusement park are the mechanical contraptions that require participation, not just spectators. The presence of rides, in fact, is the primary characteristic that distinguishes an amusement park from a tourist attraction. Audience and activity merge. Patrons participate in the spectacle in intimate ways. In fact, it has been said that on some "amusement" rides, we pay to have done to us that, which if delivered gratis but against our will, would be considered assault.

The patent applications for amusement devices made to the U.S. Patent Office in Washington D.C. number in the hundreds of thousands. Many were never built. Others were for rides that were tried once, and then abandoned. Still others operated for a time, but because they became outmoded, they, too, disappeared. Unfortunately, many rides have been lost to antiquity, with postcards and unidentified photographs all that is left to remind us that these rides even existed. Yet hundreds (if not thousands) of rides have stood the test of time. With the exception of the roller coaster (next chapter), this is their story.

Round and round we go

CAROUSELS

It is doubtful that many carousel riders realize that they are performing an ancient ritual as they ride their wooden steed in pursuit of the brass ring. In fact, few ring machines still exist to offer the opportunity to win a free ride by capturing a brass ring.

The origin of the carousel is unknown, but its ancestors are likely to have developed simultaneously in different parts of the world. However, the derivation of the word "carousel" is known. Italian and Spanish crusaders discovered a serious Arabian equestrian game and called it "little war." *Garosello* in Italian and *carosella* in Spanish, the French changed the character of the game into a lavish display of horsemanship and named it carrousel. As a result of the most famous game of carrousel, conducted by Louis XIV, the Place du Carrousel with its Arc du Carrousel to this day remains one of Paris' most visited tourist attractions. The aspect of the game of carrousel that became commemorated in the carousel ride was the ring-spearing tournament, where a lance-wielding horseman would attempt to spear a ring suspended from a tree by brightly colored ribbons. In the late 1600s, the carrousel became mechanical, with wooden horses and chariots suspended by chains from radial arms extending from a center pole. Over the next 200 years, the game of carrousel slowly evolved into the amusement device that we now know as a carousel or, in layman's terms, merry-go-round.

In America, crude carousels appeared in the mid 1800s at the resorts of New York's Vauxhall Gardens and Jones Woods, and in New Jersey at Long Branch. The first patent in America for improvements to the "flying horse," as it was often called, was granted in 1850.

In 1860, Gustav A. Dentzel arrived in the U.S. from Germany to open a cabinet shop in Philadelphia. The Dentzel family in Germany had been building carousels for years, and it wasn't long before Gustav decided to test America's reaction to a small carousel. After enthusiastic public response, Gustav repainted his shop sign

Carousel, Kiddieland, Melrose Park, Illinois

The kids enjoying a spin on the carousel at Kiddieland in the western suburbs of Chicago in 1983 are all adults now, but you can be certain they fondly remember their ride. OTTO P. DOBNICK

to read: "G. A. Dentzel, Steam and Horsepower Caroussell Builder–1867." Dentzel began by building a carousel, finding a location, and operating it himself. When he was convinced that he had established a good location, he would hire a crew to operate his ride and return to Philadelphia to build more. It is likely that selling carousels supplied the capital needed to build and place rides for his own operation, making the operations end of the business extremely profitable.

Besides being first in America, Gustav Dentzel's biggest contribution to the art of the carousel would be the number of significant wood carvers whom he trained and nurtured, including his son William. "Hobby Horse Bill," as his friends called him, not only designed and built Gustav's favorite carousel, but continued the company's tradition when Gustav died in 1909. When William himself passed away in 1928, the Dentzel factory closed. Fortunately, six decades of producing magnificent machines left sufficient numbers such that the ravages of another seven decades have not been able to obliterate. Fine examples of the vision, artistry, and craftsmanship of Gustav Dentzel can still be ridden today.

The next of the purveyors of musical roundabouts to appear on the scene were C. W. F. Dare and Charles I. D. Looff. Both began carving in the early 1870s, and both located their companies in Brooklyn, New York, virtually a brass ring's throw from one another. Whether by design, or just because they were simple and light, Dare built carousels that usually traveled with carnivals. Probably due to their transient nature, only a couple of Dare carousels still exist. They are especially significant, however, because they are of the "flying horse" type, where the rider swings outward as the carousel picks up speed. Looff's first two carousels appeared at nearby Coney Island. Eventually Looff moved his operation to California, where he built not only carousels, but complete amusement enterprises as well. Many of his carousels are still circling the globe, with a fine example going round at the Santa Cruz Beach Boardwalk in California.

Allen Herschell had a long and prosperous career as a carousel builder, beginning with his Steam Riding Gallery in 1883. Named for the place they were produced, the Tonawanda machine used wheels under its gallery rather than supporting the entire carousel on its center pole. Herschell built machines of all sizes, but became known for his small portables. Through the years, the changing company operated as the Armitage Herschell Company, Herschell-Spillman, Spillman Engineering, and the Allen Herschell Company. The company lasted into the second half of the twentieth century, and the original factory in North Tonawanda, New York, is now the Herschell Factory Carrousel Museum.

One of the most significant ride builders of the twentieth century, William F. Mangels, got his start at the end of the nineteenth century building and modifying carousels. Of significance to carousels was an improvement to the jumping mechanism he patented in 1907. In 1910, to replace the Looff ride that had been partially destroyed by fire, Mangels produced the famous Feltman carousel at Coney Island, using Marcus Charles Illions as his figure carver.

With all the carousel production in the East, and orders coming in from all over the country, Charles W. Parker saw an opportunity, and opened the Parker Carnival Supply Company in Abilene, Kansas. Located across the railroad tracks from the Eisenhower homestead, the factory is said to have employed a young Dwight D. when he was a teenager. The moving of the Parker factory to Leavenworth coincided with the golden era of Parker's career. Even the larger facility could not house the production, and at one point, seven of Parker's jumping horse "Carry-Us-All's," as Parker called them, were in various stages of completion—on the factory roof!

A late arriver to the carousel scene, Philadelphia Toboggan Company was founded in 1903. While the name belies their true intent, PTC would become the most important producer of serious whirling machines for the next 30 years. Started by businessmen who had begun to dabble in amusement parks, rather than carvers, they set out to build the most exquisite rides available. Lavish crestings, beautiful horses and ornate chariots were produced by the finest craftsman that PTC could find. A testament to their success is the fact that nearly three quarters of a century after their last carousel was installed, there are

more of PTC's in operation than any other producer. A fine example of their largest model, of which only four were built, is the five abreast Riverview Carousel from Chicago, now restored at Six Flags Over Georgia in Atlanta.

Stein & Goldstein of Brooklyn, New York, built the largest carousels ever. With as many as six horses abreast, they could seat as many as 100 riders. Although a few of their smaller rides still exist, none of the large ones are known to have survived the years.

Many small carousel companies have little in the way of machines remaining today to remind us of their existence. Fortunately they were often master carvers that left their respective marks on many of the big carousel producers. Albert and Daniel Mullers were literally raised in Dentzel's factory after their father died. They went on to produce horses for PTC as well as their own. M. C. Illions and Charles Carmel both worked for Looff before venturing out on their own. Even Solomon Stein and Harry Goldstein were paying their dues working at Mangel's Carousel Works when they met.

At the turn of the twentieth century, numerous small companies and individuals were building carousels. Many of their names are long forgotten. Others exist only on paper or in private collections. Among those names that appear occasionally are The American Merry-Go-Round & Novelty Company: the Bungarz Steam Wagon & Carrousele Works; E. Joy Morris Carousel Company; Norman & Evans; Owen & Margeson; Gillie, Godard & Company; and Fred Dolle.

The most significant variation on the carousel was the *Racing Derby*, designed by Prior & Church, of roller coaster fame. Created in the early 1920s, the sleek horses were carved by Illions. Similar to a carousel motion, four abreast horses moved up and down as well as forward and backward in relation to each other while circling at a much higher rate of speed than their carousel cousins. Of the four that were built, three

Carousel, Kennywood Park, Pittsburgh, Pennsylvania

FACING PAGE: Located near the center of the older portion of Kennywood Park, the carousel and its band organ provide an ambiance that harkens to earlier times. Carousels such as this Dentzel product are always a big draw for people of all ages, even if they don't actually climb aboard to ride. Many carousel installations feature perimeter, off-ride seating (Seabreeze Park in Rochester once offered wooden rocking chairs) for observers mesmerized by the spin of the ride and the soul-tingling beat of the band organ—a must for a true carousel experience. THREE PHOTOS, MIKE SCHAFER

Carousel detail, Kennywood Park,

The amount of artistry that went into many carousels was nothing shy of amazing. In addition to intricate sculpturework, ornate painting and colorwork speaks of a time when such details as this jester face on the Kennywood carousel were integral to the ride's personality. OTTO P. DOBNICK

still exist, two of which can be ridden, at Playland, Rye, New York, and Cedar Point, Sandusky, Ohio.

By the time the Philadelphia Toboggan Company was installing its last carousel, in 1932, the market for new wooden-horse carousels was dead. Most of the big names had already gone out of business. The Allen Herschell Company was now making horses out of aluminum to satisfy the rigors of the carnival business. Mostly, the Great Depression was taking its toll on parks, and beautiful used rides were plentiful.

Over the following half century, many carousels would be lost to fire and neglect. By the 1980s, carousel horses became so collectible that the rides were being dismantled to be sold piecemeal. Nowadays, it is hard to justify keeping a significant work intact and the cost of upkeep and insurance required to operate a classic carousel. Fortunately there are those who believe it's worth it.

There is a demand for new carousels once again, and there are also at least a dozen companies willing to answer the demand. All, however, are of the aluminum or fiberglass variety, and, unfortunately, the artistry has been lost.

CIRCLE SWINGS AND KIN

Besides the carousel, there have been innumerable rides that go round and round in one way or another. One of the most prolific of the twentieth century was the circle swing. Introduced at Coney's Luna Park in 1903, it consisted of an 80-foot tall tower from which six to eight coaches—seating four to eight riders each—were swung in a circle. Designed and built by Harry G. Traver (of later extreme roller coaster fame) the circle swing appeared at virtually every amusement park of reasonable size around the world. In keeping up with the times, the basket-like coaches were replaced in the 1920s with seaplanes, and later with large chrome rocket ships (facing page). Few examples exist today, but the ride has been recreated in the Paradise Pier area of Disney's new California Adventure theme park in Anaheim, California.

Besides its famous roller coasters, Traver Engineering went on to manufacture a number of other successful rides, including the *Caterpillar*, *Merry Mix Up*, *Auto Ride*, and *Laff in the Dark*, but his most successful ride was one he did not design. The *Tumble Bug*, also known as the *Bug* or *Turtle Chase*, was manufactured and distributed by Traver Engineering. Three to six cars (bugs or turtles) undulate around a 100-foot diameter track. A fine example named the *Turtle* still goes round and round in the

Double-deck carousel, Great America, Chicago

Twice the fun and twice the height, the double-deck carousel at what is today's Six Flags Great America between Chicago and Milwaukee is a park centerpiece, and one of the first attractions patrons see as they enter the main gate. OTTO P. DOBNICK

Circle Swing, Dorney Park, Allentown, Pennsylvania

ABOVE: Circle swings were once the staple of every amusement park worthy of its name, although they and their descendants are shunned now by today's park management on account of relatively low capacity. But economics probably aren't on the minds of these riders of Dorney Park's circle swing in 1982; they're just enjoying a breezy respite from summer's heat. OTTO P. DOBNICK

Circle Swing, Euclid Beach, Cleveland

This 1960s view of the Traver-built circle swing at Euclid Beach, Cleveland, Ohio, reveals the ride's classic lines. Although coach styles have varied since the ride was introduced in 1903, they are best remembered for their Buck Rogers rocket ships, as shown here. JAMES P. MARCUS

public interest. Today, many of the big popular rides are from Italy, Germany and the Netherlands. These manufacturers have also begun to reintroduce modern versions of classic rides. One of the true American success stories is the Tilt-A-Whirl. Built by Minnesota-based Sellner, it has been around for decades and is a staple of traveling carnivals and permanent amusement parks alike. The Tilt-A-Whirl is as popular as ever, and is the only ride Sellner makes.

REINVENTING THE WHEEL

Going round in a vertical manner has been as popular as the horizontal for almost as long. The wooden pleasure wheel traces it ancestry to the waterwheels used for irrigation in ancient times. In fact, some early pleasure wheels were powered by attached buckets fed by an adjacent stream.

In America, the wheel-as-ride idea began to make the rounds in 1867 when Issac N. Forrester, of Bridgeport, Connecticut, received a patent for his *Epicycloidal Diversion*, which he subsequently operated in Atlantic City. But it was the monumental effort at the 1893 Columbian Exposition that really got things spinning.

At 50 cents a ride, almost 1.5 million fairgoers rode George Ferris' wheel that summer and fall. From that single magnificent example, an entire industry was spawned. Almost imme-

Flying Circus, Venice, California

Looking like a circle swing on steroids, the Flying Circus at Venice Pier (Chapter 3) was probably one of the more outrageous aerial rides the amusement industry has seen. Four mammoth steel arms attached to a rotating 65-foot center tower carried free-swinging airplane coaches. Compressed air enhanced the arm movement, providing the effect of being in a dive-bombing plane. COURTESY JEFFREY STANTON

Whip, Riverview Park, Chicago

"Laugh your troubles away!" was one of the familiar jingles associated with Chicago's Riverview Park, and these two women should be trouble-free by the time their ride on the Whip is over. The cars on this ride, which could be found in varying sizes at parks throughout the country, were swept around an oval track. The leverage on the pull mechanism was such that it whipped the cars out around turns. COURTESY RALPH LOPEZ AND DEREK GEE, SHARPSHOOTERS PRODUCTIONS, INC.

front yard of the *Thunderbolt* roller coaster at Kennywood Park outside Pittsburgh.

Once established as a carousel builder, William Mangels set about to become one of the greatest ride designers and builders in America. One of his first rides, the *Tickler*, was the talk of the town when it opened at Coney's Luna Park. As early as 1912 he installed a wave making machine in the swimming pool at Palisades Park in New Jersey. But the ride for which he'll be remembered most is the *Whip*.

Through the years, manufacturers of amusement rides have come and gone with the tides of

diately following the fair, the Phoenix Iron Works of Pittsburgh began building 150-foot wheels. Of particular significance, though, was a visitor to the fair by the name of William E. Sullivan.

Sullivan was a bridge builder by trade and a mechanical tinkerer by compulsion. Upon riding the big wheel and examining the workings thoroughly, Sullivan returned home and announced to his wife that he intended to design and build a portable Ferris wheel. By 1900, he had built a prototype, the 45-foot tall "Big Eli." By 1905, with mechanical development and market testing done, he formed the Eli Bridge Company. The

Tilt-A-Whirl, Elitch Gardens, Denver

It is one of the most common and popular "flat" rides found at both traditional and theme parks and in traveling carnivals as well—Sellner's Tilt-A-Whirl. Of course, the ride isn't flat at all, or it wouldn't work. The ramping causes the cars to spin—sometimes madly, and often in relation to the weight of the occupants. A good ride operator can manipulate the speed of the ride to maximize the spinning of selected cars. The basketlike car backs are quite necessary, as the centrifugal force will pull hats and other things right off the riders. This Tilt-A-Whirl stood in front of famous Mister Twister roller coaster at the original Elitch Gardens in Denver. MIKE SCHAFER

Satellite, Lakeside Park, Denver

Only a few blocks away from the old Elitch Gardens, riders at Lakeside Park are getting their grins and spins as well. The Satellite ride allows individual riders to control the altitude of their own plane. In the background is a Ferris wheel gone awry: the Rock-O-Plane OTTO P. DOBNICK

Early Ferris wheel

Riders on an early—and rather spindly—Ferris wheel at Robinson Park (location unknown) ham it up for the photographer circa 1910. AUTHOR'S COLLECTION

Classic Ferris wheel, Whalom Park, Lunenberg, Massachusetts

Ferris wheels offer a brief respite from more harrowing rides. Whalom Park's Big Eli wheel (note brand name on rear of seats) is meticulously maintained and colorfully painted. OTTO P. DOBNICK

stockholders felt that if the Ferris wheel was not a long-term product, the company could return to bridge building. They needn't have worried. By 1952 the company, based in Jacksonville, Illinois, had built wheel No. 1000. Eli Bridge Company is now in the hands of the fourth generation of Sullivans, and the Big Eli has become the most recognized Ferris wheel model in the world. As a side note, Eli Bridge also makes one of the most popular flat rides of all time, the *Scrambler*.

For spinning vertically and adding an upside-down twist, the rides of Eyerly Aircraft can't be beat. Designed as portable rides, the *Loop-O-Plane*, *Roll-O-Plane*, and *Rock-O-Plane* found

their way into amusement parks all over the country. Although Eyerly has disappeared, their rides remain extremely popular.

For that Ferris-wheel-to-the-extreme experience, no one has ever bettered Oklahoma-based Chance Rides. The old *Swooper* and the newer *Sky Wheel* look like demented versions of the traditional Ferris wheel. The *Skydiver*, *Tumbler*, *Turbo*, and *Rampage*, are just plain wacky. But for sheer terror, the *Zipper*—wherein riders spin in caged seating that itself revolves around a huge oblong arm that itself is revolving—is the ultimate. Actually, the name of the company should be scary enough.

Double your pleasure, double your fun . . .

. . . with a Ferris wheel that's double hung. If one Ferris wheel is great, then two, of course, must be twice as good—especially if you combine them into one ride. When two wheels are hung on a giant arm that also rotates, the Ferris wheel takes on a whole new attitude. Suddenly, the gentle, predictable, and mildly exhilarating rotation of a single-wheel ride becomes a blur of confusing motion whose speed varies. This double Ferris wheel is at the now-closed Rocky Point Park in Rhode Island. OTTO P. DOBNICK

Skydiver, Rocky Point, Rhode Island

The Skydiver brought a new twist to Ferris wheeling, with enclosed coaches that spin so that, at some points, riders are looking straight down at the ground as though they were dive-bombing. OTTO P. DOBNICK

Shoot-the-Chutes

In this early twentieth century view at White City, Denver (today's Lakeside Park), it appears that spectators are having as much fun watching the Shoot-the-Chutes as the folks who are riding it. Crowds line not only the landing lagoon, but the bridge over the base of the chutes. AUTHOR'S COLLECTION

Water, water everywhere

CHUTE FOR THE STARS

The roller coaster has, for almost as long as it has existed, been known as the "King of the Park." Claims have been made to bestow the title of Queen, however, on both the carousel and Ferris wheel. Actually, the carousel would make more sense as "Prince of the Park," since it involves horses, but there was a time that another attraction vied for title to the throne—a ride called the Shoot-the-Chutes.

The *Shoot-the-Chutes* (known just as the chutes to his close friends) was not invented by Captain Paul Boyton, but he is credited for making it successful. Its 1895 debut coincided with the opening of Boyton's Sea Lion Park at Coney Island. After being transported to the top of a steep incline, a dozen passengers would board a flat-bottomed boat, and begin a fast, wet descent toward a lagoon. A carefully engineered upturn at the bottom of the ramp would send the boat skipping across the surface. In gondola fashion, a pilot standing at the back of the boat, would guide the vessel back to the landing.

When Thompson & Dundy took over Sea Lion Park to create their masterpiece Luna Park, the chutes was the only attraction deemed worthy of their park. Not only was it highlighted as the centerpiece of the new park, it was destined to start a major trend. Within a few years, the *Shoot-the-Chutes* (or similar names) would be the centerpiece of amusement parks from coast to coast. From neighboring Dreamland the following year, to virtually every Luna Park copy, White City, and Electric Park across the landscape, the *Shoot-the-Chutes* would dominate the center of the park's midway.

By the end of World War II, the novelty had worn off, and all but a few had disappeared, usually along with their corresponding parks. There were exceptions, of course. At Chicago's Riverview Park, for example, the classic 1907-built *Shoot-the-Chutes* operated for 60 years, right to the park's closing.

In the late 1980s, the *Shoot-the-Chutes* concept was rediscovered. This time, fiberglass boats make a plunge down a steep watery trough, but in this New Age version there are no upturns at the bottom. Instead, the boat creates a wall of water that not only drenches the passengers, but unsuspecting onlookers as well. With names like *Tidal wave*, *Splashwater Falls*, and *Tsunami*, over half a dozen firms are competing yearly to introduce the tallest, steepest, or wettest chutes rides. At venerable Kennywood Park, a new Shoot-the-Chutes patterned to look and operate like those popular at

the turn of the twentieth century, serves as the centerpiece for the new Lost Kennywood section.

DOWN BY THE OLD MILL STREAM

The *Canals of Venice* was a water ride invented by Arthur Pickard, of London. A serpentine course, on level ground, consisted of a narrow, shallow, water-filled canal with a dozen two-passenger boats. Motor-driven propellers mounted in the water caused the boats to drift slowly through the canal. The decade following its 1891 introduction, saw several installations in America.

The *Old Mill*, designed by George W. Schofield, was installed at Sea Lion Park in 1902. Drawing upon the grist mill as inspiration, a powered waterwheel at the entrance would add theming, as well as supply the current necessary to propel the boats. The ride would consist of a continuous-loop water trough like the *Canals of*

Mill chute ride, Coney Island, Cincinnati

Like peanut butter and chocolate, when you cross a Shoot-the-Chutes with a Tunnel of Love, you get a great combination. The resulting "mill chutes" offered thrills in the dark—either of the riders' own doing or through animated tableaus along the route—and an exhilarating splash-down that cooled off any over-activated libidos. Mill chute rides took on many names. Here at Cincinnati's Coney Island it was known as the Lost River. The winding tunnel is plainly evident in this 1970 view, as well as the lift hill to the splash-down track. DAVID P. OROSZI

Venice, through which gondola-like boats would float. The big difference was that most of the canal consisted of dark tunnels with strange scenery designed to startle the riders as they drifted by. This was the beginning of a genre fondly referred to as a "dark ride." The darkness became a big draw for romantically inclined couples looking for a little intimacy in a time when any public display of affection was frowned upon. Eventually, this became the primary reason for the ride's very existence, and most were renamed the *Tunnel of Love*. Most of these rides are now gone, although a fine example, renamed the *Old Mill* recently (in commemoration of its 100th anniversary in 2001), still flows romantically at Pittsburgh's Kennywood Park.

The Philadelphia Toboggan Company later combined the *Old Mill* with the *Shoot-the-Chutes*, and called it the *Mill Chute*. The boats would pass through the serpentine tunnels, then were drawn to the top of an incline. Typically, the boats would then break out into the sunlight, slide rapidly down into a pool, and drift back to the starting point. Although the boats have been replaced and updated over the years, one may still experience this ride, under the name of *Over the Falls* at Seabreeze in Rochester, New York.

The basic concept of these rides lives on in the fiberglass-troughed log-flume rides that have become so popular at theme parks. Arrow Development (now Arrow Dynamics) in Mountain View, California, was responsible for many of the ride mechanisms used in the attractions at Disneyland in the 1950s and 60s. Arrow's success spawned the log flumes that first appeared in the early 1960s at Six Flags Over Texas and Cedar Point. Before long, every amusement and theme park had to have one, and some even replaced their *Mill Chute*. The major difference between the new flumes and the old mills, is that the flumes are generally not dark rides and they run much faster. Two notable exceptions are the *Timber Mountain Log Ride* at Knott's Berry Farm, and Splash Mountain at Disneyland. Considered to be two of the best of the log flumes ever built, both are mostly enclosed and heavily themed.

Rattlesnake Rapids, Lagoon Park, Salt Lake City, Utah

The water-rapids ride was the next logical step in the evolution of the mill-chute ride, and they have become extremely popular at traditional and theme parks. These rides simulate a whitewater rapids river down which tublike boats sweep along with the current. At selected locations, the pleasant drift becomes a wild spin down a section of rapids. An obligatory trip past a waterfall almost always drenches at least some of the riders in the boat, as is the case with these water-dodgers at Lagoon's rapids ride in 2000.

YOU AUTO RIDE THIS

At the turn of the twentieth century, horseless carriages were still a novelty. In fact, in 1900, only 10,000 automobiles existed in all of America, and most were in the hands of those wealthy enough to afford them. Certainly the average amusement park patron did not own one. So, when rides appeared where everyday people could pilot a vehicle around a track, they became very popular indeed.

Among the first such rides was a precursor of the Dodgem called the Witching Waves, appearing at Coney's Luna Park around 1905. Patron-steered Dodgem-like cars were propelled around an oval by the undulating motion of the metal floor. Soon, auto rides increased in number and realism with small lifelike cars propelled around an elaborate track by either gasoline engines (the most realistic), or electric rail (the most controllable). Eventually, the complexity and cost of such rides, combined with an increasing population driving the real thing, drove the rides into oblivion.

Several things kept driving alive in amusement parks however, chief among them being not driving, but crashing. Bumper cars like Dodgem and Scooter have enjoyed a popularity that to this day has never waned. Like the Witching Waves before them, bumper cars consist of multiple two-passenger vehicles with big rubber bumpers, riding on a metal floor. Each car has its own electric motor, fed by an overhead grid,

Bumper car ride, Lakeside Park, Denver

A perennial favorite at amusement parks, bumper-car rides vent emotions that could otherwise lead to road rage. Or maybe it's the other way around? MIKE SCHAFER

through an electric shoe attached to a pole on the back of each car. The signs at the entrance to these rides instruct the drivers to pilot their cars in a specific direction and not to ram other drivers. Yeah, right! Everyone knows that the object is to hit someone else before they hit you. They wouldn't call it Dodgem if someone wasn't expected to be headed at you.

Racing is another reason for the continued interest in diminutive driving. Go-Kart tracks have been popular now for several decades,

and don't show any signs of slowing down. History may be another reason, as many modern parks include rides with cars similar to what your great grandparents may have driven. Undoubtedly though, the real reason that drive-yourself rides are so popular still, is that every kid wants to take a carefree cruise on the open road, all by himself. And there seems to be enough kid in all of us to keep Disneyland's Autopia as one of the most popular rides at the park for years to come.

Midget Autopia, Disneyland, Anaheim, California

The author learns to drive at Disneyland in 1965 as an attendant nearby gives a wax job to little autos awaiting the next driver. WENDELL SAMUELSON

Laff in the Dark, Crystal Beach, Ontario

Traver Engineering is best known for roller coasters, but the company produced several other memorable rides as well, one of them a ride-through attraction known as Laff in the Dark. One of the last-surviving Laff in the Darks could be found at the now-defunct—and sorely missed—Crystal Beach amusement park eight miles west of Buffalo, New York.
OTTO P. DOBNICK

Keeping park patrons in the dark

Dark rides have undergone numerous changes in the last hundred years. While they started as water rides with dark tunnels, they have evolved into tracked rides in enclosed buildings with elaborate theming. Nowadays, any enclosed attraction in which patrons ride aboard guided (usually by a track) vehicles that activate lighting and/or scenes of animation is generally considered a dark ride. True darkness is usually reserved for that sub-genre called the scary dark ride.

Scary dark rides are universally the most popular of ride-through attractions, and they trace back to the startling stunts that were a staple in the early Old Mill rides. Through the years, the scary dark rides mutated into things with names like *Dante's Inferno*, *Castle of Terror*, *Lost River*, and *Zombie*. Often they have grown from simply startling to outright grotesque.

In our desensitized modern society, most of the rides found in parks today are only startling in their humor. The best dark rides today are found in the Disney and Universal Studios parks. With their big budgets, they can create animated dinosaurs that are truly frightening. Beginning with dark rides like *Snow White's Adventure* or *Mr. Toad's Wild Ride*, Disney has a history of great dark rides. Many believe *Pirates of the Caribbean* and the *Haunted Mansion* to be the two finest dark rides ever created.

Not that these two industry leaders have a monopoly on fun dark rides. In the genre of classic, rollicking amusement park dark rides, several traditional parks offer some real trips. Knoebels Amusement Park in east central Pennsylvania has a haunted house ride-through with a supremely startling and effective conclusion—and it's just as startling for repeat riders. We wouldn't dare reveal the trick to you potential first-time riders.

A new twist in dark rides are those that are participatory. Riders board cars that are equipped with laser guns. The trick is to ward off menacing attackers along the route of the vehicle. If your laser guns strikes the target, you win points. At the end of the ride, you compare your scores with that of your seat partners'.

Disneyland's Haunted Mansion

Among the most spectacular dark rides ever created is the Haunted Mansion at Disneyland in California and Walt Disney World in Florida. The elaborate attraction, a minor portion of which is a walk-through, features illusions that are outright astonishing. In this memorable scene, a very animated "ghost" plays the organ as a transparent head floats about above the spectacle. The ride even takes riders "outside" through a nighttime cemetery scene teeming with otherworldly spirits. The ride concludes with "ghosts" joining riders in their carriages. ©DISNEYLAND

Disneyland's Pirates of the Caribbean

Hardcore Disneyland fans will argue forever as to which is better: the Haunted Mansion or Pirates of the Caribbean. Perhaps more whimsical than scary, Pirates of the Caribbean is nonetheless a remarkable achievement in dark rides, with colorful animation that transports riders back 300 years. ©DISNEYLAND

The Miniature Railway, Venice, Cal.

Venice, California's, Miniature Railway

The exquisite miniature trains at the newly opened "Venice of America" near Santa Monica, California (Chapter 3) were more than amusement rides—they were transportation options. Patrons could use the ample-size trains to travel between their hotel and other area attractions, including the famous Race Thru the Clouds roller coaster. All three locomotives—accurate renditions of early twentieth century prototypes—are still in existence. AUTHOR'S COLLECTION

Miniature Train Company streamliner, Green Bay, Wisconsin

Miniature Train Company of Rensselaer, Indiana, dominated the amusement-park train market after World War II with its line of handsome little "diesel" (actually gasoline-powered) streamliners. Painted in the colors of hometown railroad Chicago & North Western, the MTC train of Bay View amusement park at Green Bay, Wisconsin, skims the shore of Green Bay in 1987. The train has since been updated with the colors of a newer railroad in town, the Wisconsin Central. OTTO P. DOBNICK

There's just something about a train

Like the monorail, the miniature train made its public appearance at Philadelphia's Centennial Exposition of 1876. According to some accounts, as many as 14 different miniature railroads ran at the fair. Before long, this diminutive form of railroading was appearing at amusement areas all over the country.

These early trains were powered by real steam locomotives that had been scaled down to kid-sized proportions. Some of the best examples of these ran at New York's Coney Island and the House of David in Michigan. The Cagney brothers' Miniature Railway Company of Niagara, New York, was one of the earliest commercial endeavors to produce miniature locomotives and trains for exhibitions and amusement parks.

Among the finest examples of early miniature trains were the three steam locomotives that ran at Venice, California, pulling trains of tourists between the hotel and the amusement areas. All three still exist, and one is being refurbished to operate at Vasona Park in Los Gatos, California. Probably the finest example of these workhorse engines still operating on a regular schedule is at Lakeside Park, Denver, Colorado. Lakeside's wood-burner originally straddled the rails at the 1904 World's Fair in St. Louis, and though it only runs on weekends during the season, it's well worth the trip for that wonderful view of the park from across Lake Rhoda. Another excellent live-steam miniature train operation can be experienced on selected days at Kiddieland in Chicago's western suburbs. When the steam train is not in operation, the park's vintage—and spotlessly maintained (like the rest of the

park)—Miniature Train Company "diesel" streamliner does the honors.

Miniature Train Company of Rensselaer, Indiana, built most of post-World War II amusement park trains. Its most popular line was that of a modern passenger train, based on actual prototype locomotives from General Motors and passenger car copies of Pullman-Standard rolling stock. MTC's standard paint scheme for its miniature streamliners was Southern Pacific's famous red-and-orange "Daylight" livery, but a few parks had custom paint jobs done to represent local railroads. Although appearing as diesel streamliners, MTC "diesels" were in fact powered by common gasoline engines. Chance Manufacturing Company (now Chance Rides, Inc.) bought the rights from MTC sometime in the 1960s. In terms of amusement park trains, Chance is more known, however, for its *C. P. Huntington* "steam" locomotive. It had but one set of driving wheels, which was not at all like any common prototype, and is at best a caricature of an early steam locomotive. Interestingly, under this gaudy steam-locomotive cowl is none other than the same GM diesel-type trucks power mechanism that had been used on the MTC streamliners. The big drive wheel was strictly for looks.

When it came to real steam engines, Crown Metal Products was the king. Available in 15-, 16-, 24-, and 36-inch gauges, real steam power was not only the most realistic, but the most expensive. When the big theme parks like Six Flags Over Texas, started looking for trains that made an impression, Crown's 36-inch gauge was the ticket.

Walt Disney—very much the rail aficionado—originally offered to buy the Venice locomotives to run at Disneyland, but decided he wanted something more life-sized. When he couldn't find something suitable, his own staff built them. Walt had built a miniature railroad, called the Carolwood Pacific, in his backyard. The locomotive was one-eighth scale, patterned after the classic 4-4-0 (four pilot wheels, four driving wheels, no trailing wheels) engines that dominated real railroading in the nineteenth century. Walt's crew used the same design, but scaled it to five-eighths of normal size. When Disneyland opened, it had two brand new trains, exactly to Walt's liking. A few years later however, Disneyland needed more train capacity. Upon searching the countryside, Disney found an old Baldwin narrow-gauge locomotive that fit Disneyland's track perfectly. With a new boiler, rebuilt chassis, and new trim, it fit

Rocket ride, Lagoon Park, Salt Lake City, Utah

There seems to be no shortage of new ideas for new rides. At Farmington, Utah, near Salt Lake City, a traditional park by the name of Lagoon has ventured into rides very untraditional, such as its Rocket high ride. This ride has been gaining wide popularity at parks throughout North America and is appearing under a number of different names. Passengers can take their choice of either being catapulted to the top of the tower at high speed, then gently "floated" back to earth; or they can choose the cars that are hoisted to the top and then jettisoned downward, leaving stomachs dangling somewhere in outer space.

right in with its newer siblings. Since it cost half the price of the engines built from scratch, it's not surprising that a year later, when Disneyland needed a fourth, they reconditioned another old Baldwin. Since that time, many old locomotives have found new lives and new homes in theme parks all over the world.

Cyclone, Lakeside Park, Denver

This classic coaster at Denver's remarkable Lakeside Park has been thrilling riders since it opened in 1940. In 1982, one of the Cyclone's sleek trains swoops through the ride's twister section. MIKE SCHAFER

Scream Machine, Wildwood, New Jersey

FACING PAGE: This coaster name says it all! Unfortunately, this early coaster whose sign is shown in 1978, has been razed. MIKE SCHAFER

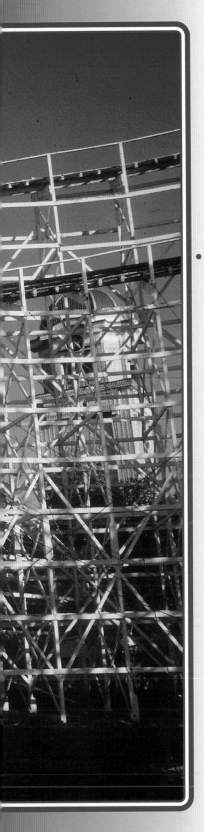

THE KING IS DEAD
Long Live the King!

The roller coaster has become the key to an amusement park's success

High speed, drastic drops, wild turns, and disorienting loops are the common elements of today's roller coaster. The humble beginnings of the gravity-powered pleasure ride go back to winter in fifteenth century Russia. But these narrow ice slides, known as "Russian Mountains," were as similar to the high-tech thrillers we enjoy today as sledding.

In the early 1800s, a wood-track, steel-wheeled ride appeared in pleasure gardens around France. These ornate attractions, referred to, among other things, as Les Montagnes Russes (again, Russian Mountains), were far

Mauch Chunk Switch Back Railway

Often cited as the first roller coaster ride in America (and America's second railroad, having opened in 1827), the Mauch Chunk-Summit Hill & Switch Back Railway—more commonly known as the Mauch Chunk Switch-Back Railway—began as a coal-hauling company. Only a couple of years later, the line was allowing passengers to ride after the daily coal runs had been made. In this scene from early in the twentieth century, a train is being pushed up the railway's second incline at Mount Jefferson. In due time, the train will be coasting along on the track underneath, on its way back down the mountain. SWITCH BACK GRAVITY RAILROAD FOUNDATION

Switchback coaster

The first coasters built expressly as amusement devices were known as "switchback" railways, because the cars rolled over a series of gentle hills from one end of the ride to the other where they reversed direction to roll back to the starting point on an adjacent track. This switchback coaster at White City in Worcester, Massachusetts, in 1906 was typical of the era. B. DEREK SHAW COLLECTION

from technologically perfect; but they were enormously popular with the daring French, and numerous incarnations sprang up. Like many trends that began in Europe, it was only a matter of time before the rides caught the eye of inventors across the Atlantic.

Some records attribute the first American roller coaster to coal-mining entrepreneur Josiah White. In 1827 he turned a coal-transport railroad at Mauch Chunk (now Jim Thorpe), Pennsylvania, into a tourist attraction. Mules hauled trains of empty mine cars along rails from Mauch Chunk to the top of Summit Hill. Under the original plan, the cars were filled with coal (and the mules!) and rolled back down the hill to be unloaded. By 1829 White had passengers taking the place of the coal in the afternoons, for 50 cents a head. Following some improvements, White's coaster made a complete loop, beginning in Mauch Chunk and climbing steeply up a 2,322-foot incline to the top of Mount Pisgah with a steam-driven cable. After completing the ascent, the car was released to begin a reportedly harrowing, mostly downhill trip back to Mauch Chunk; the entire circuit was 18 miles long. Later renamed Mauch Chunk-Summit Hill & Switch Back Railway (the "switchback" term referred to the occasional reverse in direction that cars had to make on switchback tracks during the descent), the operation lasted into the 1930s!

The term "roller coaster" is believed to have been coined in 1887 in Haverhill, Massachusetts, where a toboggan-like ride was built above an enclosed skating rink. Riders boarded toboggan sleds, which were raised, elevator style, to the top of the device. The sleds then were released onto a track comprised of hundreds of rollers and allowed to roll along the gently graded track down to the main floor. This *Roller Toboggan*, as it was named, was invented by Stephen E. Jackman and Byron B. Floyd, who also claimed to be the first to use the term "roller coaster."

Most historians, however, concur that the first authentic American roller coaster structure—one built expressly for entertainment—appeared at New York's Coney Island in 1884. The *Switch Back Railway* was designed by La Marcus Thompson, who reportedly was inspired by the namesake Mauch Chunk-Summit Hill & Switch Back Railway. Thompson's meager ride was approximately 600 feet long and stood about 50 feet tall. Riders each paid a nickel to climb aboard and enjoy the 6-MPH adventure that included a series of mild hills and valleys.

Figure 8 coaster

Not long after the continuous-circuit format was adopted for coasters by the end of the nineteenth century, the "figure 8" coaster caught on in a big way and became the big rage around the turn of the century. The format was simple but effective: Individual cars were hoisted up the lift hill and released to travel over a gently descending route, on a side-friction track that traced a figure-8 pattern back to the loading station. The Ingersoll Company built most figure-8 coasters, and they could be found coast to coast at parks of all sizes, sometimes carrying the "Figure-8" name, sometimes christened with other monikers. Only one figure-8 coaster remains in operation in North America: the recently restored Leap The Dips at Lakemont Park near Altoona, Pennsylvania. AUTHOR'S COLLECTION

Scenic Railway, Venice, California

The scenic railway-type coaster was popularized in the late 1880s. Most employed traditional railroad-type track, with flanged wheels riding on iron rails, and many were scenicked with fake mountains and tunneling trackage, as illustrated by the Venice Scenic Railway. AUTHOR'S COLLECTION

The *Serpentine Railway* appeared next at Coney, developed by Charles Alcoke. This ride differed from Thompson's version in that the course was arranged into a continuous loop. In 1885, Philip Hinkle opened Coney's third roller coaster. He further improved the ride by having passengers ride in seats which faced forward, instead of using the cumbersome park bench-like sideways seating found on earlier rides.

The traditional wooden coaster continued to evolve and improve. Thompson's *Switch Back Railway* was superseded by continuous-circuit coasters, chief among them the enormously popular Figure 8-type coasters and the "scenic railway" format. Figure-8 coasters were side-friction rides (trough-like tracks whose high sides guided coaster trains), with the track descending gently in tiers. By the turn of the century, every park worth its name had a Figure-8 coaster. Scenic railways usually employed traditional railway-type flanged wheels riding on iron rails. Just as on their larger steam-belching cousins, the flange on a coaster car's wheel acted as a natural guide wheel that steered the trains around turns. This arrangement worked fine for the relatively slow-moving, gentle, up-and-down rides where most of the track ran a straight-line course, but flat curves could not be negotiated at high speed without

Scenic Railway at Venice, Cal.

disastrous results—which is why scenic railway trains had to have a brakeman aboard to slow down trains for curves.

By contrast, the coaster cars of side-friction rides had flat (i.e., non-flanged) steel "tractor" or running wheels carrying the weight of the car, and horizontally mounted "side friction" guide

Side-friction coaster, Willow Grove Park, Philadelphia

Though not a traditional scenic railway in coaster terms, the Scenic Railway at defunct Willow Grove Park near Philadelphia does illustrate the side-friction technology that was critical to roller coaster evolution at the turn of the century. The cars rode on flangeless wheels while side-friction wheels mounted on the cars' sides kept them on course. TOM HALTERMAN

Cyclone, Coney Island, New York

The invention of the underfriction or upstop wheel circa 1912 allowed coasters to become far more wicked, with steeper drops than ever and tighter, more convoluted trackage—as vividly illustrated in this view of the yawning abyss of the 1927-built Cyclone from the top of the lift hill. MIKE SCHAFER

wheels to keep the cars on course. Upright
boards set at perpendicular angles to and on
both sides of the track formed a wooden channel
for the cars. Throughout the ride, the side-friction
wheels made contact with these upright boards
through curves and other unconventional maneuvers. Side-friction track allowed for increased
speed, especially on turns.

Side-friction technology caught on quickly and
was soon integral to most coasters, beginning
with the Figure-8 rides. Large dips and tight turns
became possible, because the cars were far less
likely to jump the track. The main drawback was
that cars moving at high speed still had a tenden-
cy to lift off the track at the apex of a short hill.
Nonetheless, one side-friction ride pushed the
envelope on the limitations of side-friction design,
and the result was the *Drop-the-Dip*. Located at
Coney Island, *Drop-the-Dip* was built in 1907 by
Christopher Feucht. He dared to design its hills to
be as steep and deep as feasible without the cars
flying off the track, and his ride was thus considered the first high-speed roller coaster.

Coaster builder John Miller almost single-hand-
edly changed all this with his inventions, the most
radical being the "upstop" or "under-friction"
wheel arrangement on a new track design: lami-
nated layers of wood that formed an upside-down
L-shaped rail that raised the trains high above the
"ties" or crossmembers. The side-friction wheels
rode against the inside edge of the L-rail and the
new under-friction (upstop) wheels extended
beneath the L-rail. When the car or train entered a
low-gravity moment out on the course, riders were
treated to some out-of-seat "airtime," but the
upstop wheels prevented the cars from completely
taking flight. This new format literally locked the
coaster cars to the track and provided the perfect
means for taking the wooden roller coaster to
much greater levels of terror. This new track
arrangement is still in use today, even on new
coasters, wood or steel track.

Among other things, the new engineering
allowed exciting variations in track layout. The
simpler "out-and-back" courses—which took riders to a far point, leaping hills and valleys and
banking turns along the route, and back again—
gave way to "twister" track plans whereby the
track circuit wrapped around itself in sharp turns,
wild drops, and harrowing curves. But to let
potential riders know that this wild new breed of
coaster featured the new under-friction wheel

Golden age twister

Early in the 1920s, the famed design team of Thomas Prior and Fred Church began creating some of the most distinctive, beautiful coasters in the history of the amusement industry. One of the few remaining P&C-inspired rides is the Giant Dipper at Belmont Park in San Diego, CA. Opened in 1925, it was an example of Fred Church's Bobs-series coasters, with a twisting track layout that occupied relatively little space. It operated (briefly renamed Earthquake) until 1976 when Belmont Park closed as an amusement center. Demolition loomed, but coaster aficionados rallied to the cause, and a reconditioned Giant Dipper reopened in 1990. It is shown in 1999.

PTC coaster, Lenape Park, West Chester, Pennsylvania

The Philadelphia Toboggan Company designed nearly 150 roller coasters between 1904 and 1975. The Brandywine Express, shown in July 1974 at Lenape Park near Philadelphia, is a PTC product of 1926, designed by Herb Schmeck, a man long associated with the company. TOM HALTERMAN

arrangement, they were sometimes referred to as "safety coasters."

During the "Roaring Twenties," ever larger and more spectacular wooden coasters lured crowds into the parks. Roller coasters were approaching the 100-foot-high mark. Drops had become steeper, turns tighter, and track layouts unpredictable to riders. Some designers built coasters that mercilessly tossed riders about as seemingly out-of-control trains flew through their circuits. The coaster-building craze reached an all-time zenith in 1928, when nearly 40 major roller coasters were constructed at parks around the country.

Those seemingly carefree and extravagant days of the 1920s came to a swift and screeching halt with the stock market crash of 1929. The ensuing Great Depression cooled the coaster fever as the U.S. economy plunged into a tailspin. World War II curtailed coaster construction even more owing to a critical shortage of construction material and manpower. Following Armistice Day in 1945, a postwar euphoria swept through America and interest in amusement parks was revitalized. Many wooden coasters were overhauled and cosmetically improved. In 1945, for example, Geauga Lake (now Six Flags Worlds of Adventure) near Cleveland renovated its superb 1926 woodie, the *Big Dipper*. In 1946, a classic which still reigns supreme opened at Hershey Amusement Park (now Hersheypark), Hershey, Pennsylvania: the *Comet*, built by Philadelphia Toboggan Company.

The arrival of the 1950s found America in a state of flux and the popularity of something called television brought a new, high-tech competitor for amusement parks. Only a few new coasters opened in the 1950s, most of them "kiddie" coasters that would introduce baby boomers to coastering.

Walt Disney was a force from that early TV era, and reportedly he was initially unwilling to consider coasters for his revolutionary park, associating them with the seediness that had skulked its way into many parks by this time. Ironically, though, Disney unwittingly played a role in a future coaster renaissance. Eventually he decided to add a coaster to Disneyland that was, in effect, disguised as something else. Ultimately it served to provide roller coasters with a new set of "work clothes."

The ride first and foremost had to meet his lofty standards of excellence: it had to be quiet, comfortable, and completely safe. Industry pioneers Carl Bacon and Ed Morgan of Arrow Development, a small California-based manufacturing firm, created a unique, all-steel track system that would change the amusement industry forever. Bacon and Morgan retained the traditional tractor/side-friction/under-friction wheel assembly design for coaster cars, but gripped them around a tubular steel rail instead. Their ingenuity resulted in Disneyland's famous *Matterhorn Bobsleds*. This historically important ride opened to the public in 1959 and was a smash hit. With its multiple low-slung bobsleds swirling down, through, and around a 147-foot-tall replica of the famous Swiss mountain peak on two different track runs, the *Matterhorn* gave Disneyland its first real thrill ride.

Based on the ultra-successful technology devised for Disneyland's *Matterhorn Bobsleds*, the next tubular-steel track roller coaster was opened at Six Flags Over Texas in 1966. The *Runaway Mine Train* in many ways mimicked the action of wooden roller coasters: passengers boarded ore-car-themed trains and embarked on a tight, twisted track layout comprised of banked curves, surprise drops, and quick directional changes. The mild ride appealed to the masses, and mine-train-type coasters began to proliferate.

So very many wonderful old amusement parks and their respective collections of vintage wooden roller coasters were lost during that long,

continued on page 107

Matterhorn Bobsleds, Disneyland, Anaheim, California

Opened in 1959 at the original Disneyland, the Matterhorn Bobsleds was a coaster disguised as a pair of bobsled runs winding through a very scaled down replica of Switzerland's famous Matterhorn Mountain. As the first successful tubular steel track roller coaster, it forever changed roller coaster design—an ironic situation considering that Walt Disney was not a big proponent of roller coasters. WENDELL SAMUELSON

Of course, the explosion in roller coaster creativity did not occur by chance. Talented and resourceful individuals made it all possible, and a quick perusal of industry history reveals a core group of names and manufacturers behind great installations. The most prolific designers imprinted their distinctive styles onto each of their rides as clearly as a fingerprint.

Known as "The Master," John Miller made his most important contribution to roller-coaster evolution in 1912: the under-friction wheel, which locked the trains to the track. The most prolific and influential designer active during the first golden age of coasters, Miller's hallmarks include deep "camelback" hills and large, flat turns. Miller rides still operating as of the new millennium included the Jack Rabbit at Pittsburgh's Kennywood Park and the Big Dipper at Six Flags Ohio near Cleveland.

A supremely talented and trailblazing engineer named Fred Church and his business partner, Thomas Prior, unified as Prior & Church to initially work with John Miller during the design and construction of designer Frederick Ingersoll's Race Thru the Clouds in Venice, California (Chapter 3). The coaster that first showcased Church's true brilliance, though, was the Whirlwind Giant Dipper that opened at Santa Monica, California in 1921. It featured severe banking, steep drops, and nonstop action and would spawn a whole family of what became known as "Bobs"-type coasters.

In 1924, Church opened his first coaster east of the Mississippi. Built by the Traver

A twisted nightmare at Wildwood, New Jersey

Designer/builder Vekoma is responsible for this devious steel inverted coaster at Morey's Pier at Wildwood. Opened in 1995, the Great Nor'easter whirls riders through a 2,150-foot course.
AUTHOR'S COLLECTION

Engineering Company in Chicago, Riverview Park's Bobs immediately outgrossed the park's numerous other coasters three to one.

Church coasters' structurework almost sang of elegance and grace, and it is apparent that he intentionally designed his rides to be picturesque as well as physically thrilling. His masterpiece? Many say it was the late lamented Aeroplane Coaster at Playland at Rye, New York.

Born in 1877, Harry Traver was also designing coasters in the early twentieth century, and will forever be known as a maverick in the amusement industry. Traver Engineering first acted as a contractor for Prior & Church, building several of their Bobs coasters. But, Traver himself is best known for his "Giant Cyclone Safety Coasters," reputedly the wildest, most violent coasters ever built. The best known of the three that were built (all in 1927)—the Cyclone at Crystal Beach near Buffalo, New York—had to have a nurse stationed near its exit.

The link between golden-age coasters and renaissance-era (1972–present) rides was John Allen. He joined the Philadelphia Toboggan

Company during the Depression and worked his way up to PTC presidency in 1954. Allen reportedly spoke out against radical coasters featuring heavily banked turns, super-elevated spiral drops, and other severe attributes. Most John Allen coasters featured a smooth ride over over classic parabolic hills. Yet, he reluctantly designed one ride that was terrifying in its own right, Mister Twister (1965–1994) at the original Elitch Gardens in Denver.

Many industry giants crossed paths under the auspices of a few key companies. Prime among them was the aforementioned Philadelphia Toboggan Company, which opened in 1904 in Germantown, Pennsylvania. Originally known for its toboggan slides and exquisite carousels, PTC's greatest achievements include approximately 140 wooden roller coasters—many of them constructed during the first golden age under the direction of Herbert Schmeck. The Wildcat at Lake Compounce in Connecticut is an excellent example of Schmeck design.

Though PTC stopped designing roller coasters when John Allen died in 1979, his legacy lived on as the coaster-design torch was handed over to civil engineer William Cobb. The soft-spoken Texan had worked with Allen on such popular rides as the Great American Scream Machine (Six Flags Over Georgia) and Screamin' Eagle (Six Flags Over Mid-America). Until his death in 1990, Cobb went on to design a series of wooden coasters that in a couple of instances were absolutely ferocious—top among them the Texas Cyclone, the first of several renaissance-era clones of the Coney Island Cyclone.

Also known as the Dayton Fun House & Riding Device Company, National Amusement Devices (NAD) was established in the 1920s and was a major player during the dismal days of the Great Depression. Though not nearly as prolific as PTC, NAD's rides and contributions were exemplary. Perhaps NAD's most recognized contribution to coasterdom was the firm's Art Deco-inspired Century Flyer rolling stock, complete with headlights.

Many coaster-building families worked during the first golden era to produce rides that drew throngs to the parks. The pioneering Vettel clan, headed by Erwin and Edward A. Vettel, entered the amusement business in the 1890s, and two notable Vettel-designed coasters are still in operation today, the Blue Streak at Conneaut Lake, Pennsylvania, and the sensual Art Deco Cyclone at Denver's Lakeside Park.

Custom Coasters of Westchester, Ohio, is a contemporary family-based firm that vigorously excels in the art of wooden roller coaster construction. Owned by Denise Dinn-Larrick—daughter of Charlie Dinn who designed the Beast at Kings Island—highly-praised CCI is without question the most prolific wooden coaster company around today. During the 1980s and 1990s, Dinn-Larrick worked on numerous coaster relocations as well as brand-new rides. Accompanied by husband Randy Larrick, brother Jeff Dinn, her father as consultant, and a crack team of designers, engineers, and builders, CCI has emerged as a dynamic force in the amusement industry with more than 25 rides to its credit during its short history.

Although Custom Coasters may be the busiest of the new wooden coaster builders, Great Coasters International (GCI), based in Sunbury, Pennsylvania, and Santa Cruz, California, has a noble mission of creating "retro-classical" coasters. Co-owners Michael Boodley (designer) and Clair Hain Jr. (builder) are clearly influenced by Fred Church, with coasters that are extraordinarily graceful and well-defined, including the Wildcat at Pennsylvania's Hersheypark (1996); Roar at Six Flags America

near Washington, D.C. (1998); and Gwazi at Busch Gardens Tampa Bay, Florida (1999).

Now retired, German-born Anton Schwarzkopf has been prominent in the steel-coaster revolution since 1964, designing and manufacturing portable installations—e.g., Jet Stars and Thrillers—and permanent rides, chief among them the Great American Revolution at California's Magic Mountain and the Mindbenders at Six Flags Over Georgia and at West Edmonton (Alberta) Mall.

Arrow Dynamics perfected tubular-steel track coasters in the late 1950s and looping coasters in the 1970s, and examples of Arrow products can be found from coast to coast. Aside from numerous early corkscrew rides, Arrow has built a number of well-liked multi-inversion coasters, including the Vortex at Kings Island, Cincinnati, and the Shock Wave at Six Flags Great America, Chicago. Arrow has furthered its fame through its hypercoasters. Two stand out: Desperado—with a 225-foot drop—near Las Vegas, Nevada, and, at Cedar Point, the wildly popular Magnum XL-200.

In 1990, a Swiss firm called Bollinger & Mabillard introduced a second-generation steel-track standup coaster and in 1992 unveiled Batman—The Ride, the first of a series of revolutionary inverted-type looping coasters with track above the cars. B&M also introduced a succession of larger stand-up and sit-down above-track looping coasters, each sporting the four-abreast seating and exceptional smoothness.

A number of companies have scrambled to hop on the inverted-coaster bandwagon, including the Dutch firm Vekoma, which went on to design Invertigo, a suspended looping shuttle coaster. Intamin also took a step into the future by marrying new linear-induction motor (LIM) technology with the inverted coaster to build coasters whose trains are launched at high speed directly into the track circuit.

No matter how wild the dream, today's designers and engineers seem to be able to transform it into reality.

Shivering Timbers, Michigan's Adventure

Off in a quiet corner of Michigan near Muskegon stands a monster wooden coaster designed by Denise Dinn-Larrick's Custom Coasters International. In part a tribute to John Miller-designed "camelback" coasters of the 1920s, the 125-foot tall Shivering Timbers opened in 1998. MIKE SCHAFER

Mister Allen's Mister Twister

One of the few great coasters to come out of the 1960s—a dismal era for parks and coasters—was Mister Twister (later simply known as Twister), which opened in the mid-1960s at the original Elitch Gardens in Denver, Colorado. It was coaster designer John Allen's most stormy creation. In this scene from 1983, a Twister train is hurtling with wild abandon through the ride's famous double helix. The ride was actually quite unlike all other John Allen rides, which normally feature large but smooth, flowing hills and flat turns. Mister Twister was consistently rated as one of the best coasters in the U.S., and in the process it helped bridge the gap between postwar park and coaster decline and the renaissance that began in the early 1970s. MIKE SCHAFER

Euclid Beach's coaster "mountain range," Cleveland

The three favorite coasters at famed Euclid Beach Park on Cleveland's east side stood side-by-side, forming a veritable barrier of wooden trestlework. At far left in this 1969 view—the park's final season—is the lift hill of the Flying Turns, a coaster whose trains careen through troughlike track to imitate a bobsled ride. The center coaster, with a train inching up the lift hill, is the wonderful Thriller, arguably the park's most popular coaster. At right is the twin-track Racing Coaster (earlier known as the Derby, Derby Racer, and Racing Derby), the park's veteran coaster, dating from 1913. JAMES P. MARCUS

Continued from page 103

unstable period between the start of the Depression and the end of 1960s. The demise of Chicago's Riverview in 1967 meant the leveling of favorites like the *Bobs*, *Fireball*, and *Flash*. When Cleveland's Euclid Beach closed in 1969, coaster fans took a similar loss: the *Thriller*, *Flying Turns*, and *Racer* would never thrill riders again. The *Cyclone Racer* at the Pike in Long Beach—one of the greatest coasters ever—also came down, in 1968. There were a few bright spots—notably Elitch Gardens' (Denver) new *Mister Twister* of the mid-1960s and Kennywood Park's fabulous *Thunderbolt* of 1968—but these were the exceptions to a decline in coasterdom.

But with 1972 came an abrupt, almost miraculous reversal in this seemingly indiscriminate wave of devastation. That year symbolized the American roller coaster's true emergence into the second golden age. The catalyst of this historically important event was the well-publicized debut of an exciting wooden coaster near Cincinnati, Ohio, called the *Racer*. Designed by Philadelphia Toboggan Company president John Allen for Kings Island, the new Cincinnati theme park, this sparkling double-tracked thriller garnered a phenomenal degree of notoriety. The *Racer*'s premier was, without question, a pivotal moment in the history of the roller coaster: it gave the amusement industry a much-needed shot in the arm in the form of the joy and incomparable excitement that only a well-designed wooden coaster could deliver. The roller coaster had been rediscovered.

In the mid 1970s, the amusement industry revisited the looping-coaster concept. Designers went to work armed with advanced mathematics, powerful computers, superior steel-bending techniques, tubular-track technology, and a determination to offer the thrill-seeking public something new and unusual. The next logical step was sending riders upside down. Initially foregoing the vertical loop concept pioneered at Coney Island at the turn of the century, engineers instead devised a barrel-roll maneuver and called the resulting ride a "corkscrew" (which is both a defining term and often the applied name of coasters of this type). This sensational coaster opened to great fanfare

The Racer, Kings Island, Cincinnati, Ohio

The coaster often credited with reviving coaster popularity is the twin-tracked Racer, opened in 1972 in the Coney Island section of the new Kings Island theme park. MIKE SCHAFER

Inverted coaster

The inverted coaster was the evolutionary step that followed the suspended coaster. Both tracks are overhead, but inverted coaster trains are firmly affixed to the wheel carriages; the coaches of suspended coasters hang freely, allowing them to swing. On the inverted coaster, Great White, at Sea World in San Antonio, Texas, in 1999, riders legs dangle in mid-air during an outside loop.

Corkscrew coaster

Once engineers had figured out how to best loop a coaster (tubular steel track was one of the keys) in a manner that was safe and comfortable for riders, a new era in coastering emerged. Early renaissance-era loopers featured a double barrel roll or "corkscrew," which became a generic name for this format. This is the Corkscrew at Michigan's Adventure in 1999. As technology improved, with the help of computers, upside-down elements or "inversions" grew ever more convoluted.

at California's Knotts Berry Farm in 1975. It was an instant success.

The first successful vertical looping coaster was built at California's Magic Mountain in 1976. This wondrous new marvel was also an immediate hit. Aptly dubbed the *Great American Revolution*, this polished thriller was a long, graceful ride and an amazing engineering accomplishment. The *Great American Revolution* even "starred" in Universal's 1977 film Rollercoaster, giving the world a glimpse of the latest word in amusement ride technology.

The introduction of the looping coasters ignited a virtual arms race of steel construction that continues to this day. In addition to growing exponentially in height and length, the number of "inversions" (segments incorporating some sort of upside-down track elements) began to increase. Fierce-sounding maneuvers like "sidewinders," "boomerangs," "cutbacks," and other stomach-churning acrobats comprised these seemingly otherworldly machines.

But not at the expense of the wooden coaster. The *Texas Cyclone*, which opened at Houston's AstroWorld in 1976, is a Texas-size version of New York's illustrious Coney Island *Cyclone*, created

after AstroWorld's plans to purchase that famous ride fell through. Hailed by many as the greatest modern wooden coaster on the planet, the *Texas Cyclone* was an over-the-top thriller extraordinaire. More wooden coasters followed suit, including the *Beast* at Kings Island, opened in 1979. With a 7,400-foot track circuit that includes not one but two lift hills, the *Beast* became—and as of the new millennium remained—the world's longest wooden roller coaster.

The dawn of the 1980s found steel-track coaster designers virtually repeating history. Like their counterparts back in the Roaring Twenties, these engineering renegades were eager to push the envelope beyond the norm, constantly challenging the unrelenting laws of gravity by devising innovative ways to scare park guests right out of their pants. Arrow was once again at the forefront when it introduced the first suspended coaster in 1982 at Kings Island. Called the *Bat*, this fascinating prototype featured seven-car trains hanging from an overhead track. The basically free-swinging four-passenger vehicles gave riders a real and sometimes frightening sample of a bat's erratic flight pattern. Unfortunately, this amazing new ride was also plagued with teething problems and after two years was dismantled in favor of a more traditional multi-looping steel coaster, the *Vortex*. Nonetheless, two examples of an improved suspended coaster opened in 1984: *The Big Bad Wolf* at Busch Gardens Williamsburg, Virginia, and *XLR8* at AstroWorld in Houston, Texas. That same year, the pioneering Kings Island opened North America's first "stand-up coaster," the *King Kobra*. The ride featured cars on which all riders stood (engaged in a harness system,

The Millennium Force, Cedar Point, Ohio

Capitalizing on a momentous point in history, the Millennium Force, true to its name, opened in 2000. An impressive 310 feet tall, the hypercoaster travels at a brain-crunching 93 MPH. COURTESY CEDAR POINT

Chang, Kentucky Kingdom, Louisville

Opened in 1997 is a splendidly themed stand-up looping coaster that turns passengers upside down five times (five egg rolls, please).

however) on open-platform cars throughout the ride, which included a vertical loop.

In 1988 Arrow Dynamics took the looping coaster to the next level. The firm built the first of three monstrous multi-looping coasters at Great America near Chicago. This ride was the biggest looping coaster to date and offered a mind-numbing seven inversions. Two similar seven-loop versions subsequently opened at Great Adventure (1989) at Jackson, New Jersey, and Magic Mountain (1990) outside of Los Angeles. Arrow went on to rock the amusement industry in 1989 by being the first ride manufacturer to achieve the elusive 200-foot high mark for a continuous-circuit roller coaster. Dubbed *Magnum XL200*, this groundbreaking steel thriller debuted at Cedar Point in Sandusky, Ohio. It earned the honor of becoming the world's very first "hypercoaster," a term designating a coaster standing 200 feet or taller. It was fashioned completely of steel, yet mimicked the traditional up-and-down track profile of the classic out-and-back wooden coaster. There are no loops or corkscrews in its track layout.

In 1992, the next step in steel-track coaster evolution took place when a cousin of the suspended coaster was born. *Batman—The Ride* was the first "inverted" coaster. Like the suspended coaster, the track was overhead. However, rather than free-swinging coaches, the coaster vehicles were rigidly fixed to their wheel assemblies. The free-swinging cars of a suspended coaster provide an exceptionally thrilling ride, but the format is not conducive to "inversion" (upside-down) acrobat-

ics; the inverted coaster is. *Batman* featured an ultra-tight layout that included two vertical loops, a zero-gravity "heartline spin," and a pair of corkscrews. However, cranking the thrill factor up another notch, the inverted coasters' floorless ski lift-like cars allow riders' feet to dangle, which dramatically heightens the sense of soaring flight. Yet another whole world opened up in coasterdom, and a new fleet of inverted coasters invaded parks from coast to coast, among them the *Raptor* at Cedar Point in 1994; *Montu* at Busch Gardens, Tampa, in 1995; and *Top Gun* at Paramount's Carowinds at Charlotte, North Carolina.

In 1996, two identical coaster systems were constructed using new linear-induction-motor technology (LIM). In essence, a long series of LIMs are placed trackside along the level launch alley (or at other points along the course where the train might require a boost). Long metal fins attached to the cars pass through the LIMs. Powered in sequence, the magnetic force generated by the LIMs propels the train. Both installations were named *The Outer Limits: Flight of Fear*. Simultaneously constructed at Paramount's Kings Dominion (near Richmond, Virginia) and Kings Island, these rides are cleverly themed around the vintage 1960s TV show, "The Outer Limits." The completely enclosed coasters feature six-car trains being launched along a flat plane from 0 to 60 MPH in three seconds. At the end of the launch corridor, the trains enter one of the tightest, most convoluted tangles of coaster track ever devised. Numerous inversions, severely banked turns, and compound curves produce a disorienting and turbulent tour of a darkened, planetarium-like building.

Meanwhile, wood-track coasters grew more popular than ever, and a whole new crop came in with the 1990s. Since its 1995 debut, everyone's been ravin' about the new, negative-G-riddled *Raven* at Holiday World near Evansville, Indiana. The *Wildcat*, at Pennsylvania's Hersheypark, opened in 1996, replicating a golden-age twister. In 1999, the gargantuan double-tracked "dueling coaster"—*Gwazi*, at Busch Gardens Tampa Bay—was launched. Opposing trains race through heart-stopping near-miss flybys. And then in 2000, Kings Island unveiled a wooden *looping* coaster, *Son of Beast*!

As the 2000s unfurl, more new woodies are in the works. There's nothing quite like a traditional wooden coaster, you know. La Marcus Thompson found that out over a century ago.

Revived golden age classic

The new Roar coaster at Six Flags Marine World at Vallejo, California, is the work of Great Coasters International, known for its "retro" rides that have revived the classic look and ride quality of lost coasters of the 1920s. Coasters have become so popular that many "non-ride" parks such as those with nautical attractions, miniature golf, or even go-karts are installing coasters.

Hoosier Hurricane, Monticello, Indiana

For years, Indiana Beach made do with a couple of modest-size, semi-portable all-steel coasters—a Galaxy ride and a Jet Star dubbed the Tig'rr. Then in 1994, the park surprised the amusement industry by opening a large wood-track coaster, the Hoosier Hurricane. Custom Coasters International built the ride over part of Lake Shafer as well as above sections of the compact park to conserve space. Although its traditional wood track gives it the feel of a classic woodie, the support structure is actually steel girders painted white. The walloping ride was joined in 2001 by yet another new wood-track coaster, the Cornball Express.

Idora Park in twilight

A string of misfortunes brought Idora Park—a gem of an amusement park at Youngstown in northeastern Ohio—to its knees, unexpectedly soon, in 1984. On a balmy evening in June 1983, Idora is aglow in neon splendor as its ultra-wild Wildcat coaster reaches into a twilight sky. OTTO P. DOBNICK

Coaster car as planter

FACING PAGE: When some parks died, their infrastructure was simply left to rot. At abandoned Lakewood Park in Atlanta, Georgia, plants have taken up residence in a Greyhound coaster car.

GREAT LOST PARKS
May They Rust in Peace

A tribute to the Palisades, Riverviews, Euclid Beaches, and the Pikes of the past

How does an amusement park earn the status of Great? Through longevity? Coney Island's Dreamland would be considered by most historians to be one of the greatest parks ever, but it lasted only seven seasons.

Size? Certainly Pacific Ocean Park at Santa Monica, California, is considered a great park, but built almost entirely on a pier over the water, it certainly didn't compare in size to Chicago's mammoth Riverview.

Popularity? Popularity is rather subjective. Popular enough to have had a book written about it? Midway

Park in western New York is a fine example of a small traditional amusement park and has been the subject of a book, but it was never comparable to the grandeur of Celoron Park to the south—the last remnant of which burned in the 1950s—and no book has chronicled the life of that park.

Certainly there will be debates over which parks were the greatest. Ambiance, location, and the quantity and quality of the rides and games are all critical factors. And of course, roller coaster fanatics are likely to choose their favorite parks based on their coaster lineup.

There has been much discussion as to why certain great parks have failed. Why would a park, after managing to survive the lean years of the Great Depression and the shortages and indifference of World War II in the '40s, finally give up during the affluent years of the '50s, '60s and '70s? Even the owner's reasons given for throwing in the towel are dubious at best. Who would admit to something as controversial as racial tensions, unless to cover-up their own fiscal incompetence? Or maybe they just got tired of competing with television and extravagant theme parks.

Selecting the parks to feature in this chapter was both easy and agonizing. We could do a whole book just on lost parks! What follows is merely a sampling of operations whose memories seem to live on with particular vividness.

Coney Island at Cincinnati, Ohio

Once an apple orchard on the shores of the Ohio River, what would become Coney Island began its entertainment era with a dancing hall, bowling alley, and a mule-powered merry-go-round. As the apple trees died out, they were replaced with the maple trees that still shade the grounds.

In 1886 two steamboat captains—William and Malcolm McIntyre—bought the land to encourage travel on their boats. Renamed Ohio Grove, "The Coney Island of the West," it officially opened on a rainy June 21, 1886. The steamer *Guiding Star* made runs to the park four times a day for a 50-cent round trip that included park admission.

The park was expanded, and in 1893 a landmark feature—Lake Como—was added. Sunlite Pool, an engineering marvel that still stands, was later installed next to it. Measuring an incredible 200 x 401 feet, it remains the largest recirculating swimming pool in the world, accommodating up to 10,000 swimmers.

As the century ended, attractions included one of the region's first movie theaters; a wooden Ferris wheel; a carousel; the *Dip the Dips* roller coaster; and Hales Tours, an early simulation of a countryside railroad trip.

The year 1913 brought Ohio River floodwaters, signaling a nemesis that would dog Coney Island to this day. By now Chester Park, both closer to Cincinnati and served by trolleys, provided heavy competition, and World War I further hurt business. As the 1920s began, Coney Island's prospects improved. Renowned roller coaster designer John Miller built the *Sky Rocket* and one of the industry's first "kiddielands" was installed, with a variety of scaled-down rides including a merry-go-round, train, and airplane swings.

One of the largest amusement parks in the country as the 1930s dawned, Coney Island had the *Wildcat*, *Twister*, and *Greyhound* coasters; the *Cascades* and *Mystic Chute* water rides; *Devil's Kitchen* and *Bluebeard's Palace* fun houses; the *Tumble Bug*, *Custer Cars*, and a great carousel.

One of the largest floods in Ohio history hit in 1937, submerging Coney Island again. Carousel horses floated away, with parts recovered as far away as Paducah, Kentucky. The park was rebuilt and did a good business in the late 1940s, with the new *Shooting Star* coaster, *Mirror Maze*, *Rocket Ships*, *Dodge-'em*, *Laff-in-the-Dark*, *Whip*, *Lost River*, and *Flying Scooters* among the line up and eight kiddie rides in the Land of Oz.

At the season peak, July 1969, while the new Log Flume was attracting record crowds, Taft Broadcasting purchased Coney Island and announced it would open Kings Island, an all-new theme park northeast of Cincinnati. Coney Island would close as an amusement park following the 1970 season. Unlike other old traditional parks that slowly faded away, Coney Island's final year was a season-long party: 2.75 million visitors turned out to say goodbye.

While the focus in 1972 was on the new park—which featured a Coney Island section whose design mimicked its namesake—old Coney Island remained somewhat lively. Since the immense Sunlite Pool could not be moved to King's Island,

38:—

GREETINGS FROM

CONEY ISLAND

CINCINNATI, OHIO

48264

Copycat, copycat . . .

. . . but the only thing that Cincinnati's Coney Island copied from its New York counterpark was the name. Coney Island was very much a highly respected, traditional amusement park beloved by the folks of southwestern Ohio and northern Kentucky. Its memory survives in the Coney Island section of nearby Kings Island theme park as well as at the original park site itself, which still serves as a picnic and swimming area.
AUTHOR'S COLLECTION

Taft continued to operate it. To make the most of its holding, Taft reopened Coney Island's sprawling picnic groves, added a private tennis club, and renamed the facility Old Coney.

In 1987, Great American Communications purchased Taft Broadcasting and Coney Island along with it. Rides were soon clustered around Lake Como again, with *Krazy Kars*, kiddie and adult *Bumper Boats*, and a Ferris wheel in operation. In 1991, a Cincinnati businessman purchased the park and renovations of Sunlite Pool and the bathhouse were completed. The Pepsi Python, a small steel roller coaster, was added in 1999, giving the park 12 major and eight kiddie rides. Although no longer the region's largest amusement facility, Coney Island retains many of its beloved traditions—swimming at Sunlite Pool, dancing under the stars in Moonlite Gardens, and strolling along the Ohio River.

Cincinnati's Coney Island

MAIN PHOTO: A lofty ride aboard the sky ride in 1970 reveals just how meticulously maintained Coney Island was, right up to the end. Note the Tumble Bug at lower right; the coaster is the Shooting Star. DAVID P. OROSZI

Skee Ball parlor, Coney Island

Fastidious landscaping, gardens surround Coney's space-age Skee Ball parlor on the mall. AUTHOR'S COLLECTION

Crystal Beach, Ontario

Hard against the lapping waves of Lake Erie, Crystal Beach was a tradition for southern Ontarians and western New Yorkers for over a century. In this 1984 perch-eye view looking northwest, the park's beloved Comet coaster defines Crystal Beach's perch on the sandy shoreline. MIKE SCHAFER

Fun City Arcade, Crystal Beach

Crystal Beach harbored some wonderful Art Deco touches that helped transport visitors back to the big band era. OTTO P. DOBNICK

Crystal Beach, Ontario

Crystal Beach began as a "Chautauqua" area, or religious campground, in 1888. The auditorium, tents, and picnic grounds proved popular enough to draw 150,000 people per season. The Crystal Beach Company took the opportunity to make money by offering side shows and refreshments between sermons; later, it installed a pier, amusements, and ferry service on Lake Erie over to nearby Buffalo, New York. The park was purchased by another ferry company in 1908.

More amusement rides were installed, including the John H. Brown-designed *Backety Back Scenic Railway* roller coaster in 1909, minus scenery though. The riverboat-like station, capped by a peaked roof and two cupolas, stood on a large boardwalk. The trains consisted of two cars with ten double seats that looked like Victorian park benches. The immensely popular ride remained in operation until 1926, and its broad acceptance led to the construction of another coaster, the *Giant Coaster*, in 1916. Only once modified, it remained in operation until the park's demise in 1989; it was one of the last few side-friction coasters in America at the time.

In 1927, the park unveiled one of Traver Engineering's legendary new *Giant Cyclone Safety Coasters*. The ferocious ride—to this day considered by some to be the most violent, fearsome roller coaster ever built—reportedly drew 5,000 riders on opening day, and eager crowds broke down a railing trying to get a closer look. Unfortunately, the high forces it generated made it a maintenance headache, and mounting costs and lack of repeat riders prompted its dismantling. Much of the steel structure was salvaged and used by the Philadelphia Toboggan Company to construct the looming—and greatly loved—*Comet* coaster in 1948, designed by James Mitchell and Herbert Schmeck. After Crystal Beach closed, the ride was sold and moved to The Great Escape in Upstate New York, where it reigns supreme to this day.

By the end of World War II, the park boasted 20 rides (including six kiddie rides), a fun house, penny arcade, shooting gallery, and picnic facilities. During 1950s, the popularity of big bands was waning, and the dance hall became less popular while park attendance dropped off as well. When ferry service from Buffalo was suspended in 1956, people were forced to arrive entirely via buses or cars, which created major traffic jams and parking problems. The net result was an even greater reduction in park attendance. Nonetheless a *Wild Mouse* steel roller coaster—all the rage in the 1950s—was added, delighting patrons for several years.

Attendance continued to languish, and in 1974 a fire severely damaged the dance hall, with the half million dollars it took to refurbish it cutting further into profits. But, more rides were added including the *Pirate Ship*, *Chair-O-Plane*, and a *Lady Bug*. In 1978 the Super Duper Mountain water slides were installed, and in the ensuing years a *Flying Bobs* and *Saw Mill River* flume ride joined the line up.

Unable to compete with other, newer, more heavily promoted parks in the region—notably Canada's Wonderland at Toronto and Marineland near Niagara Falls, which had just installed the record-breaking *Dragon Mountain* steel-track coaster—Crystal Beach faced bankruptcy in 1983. In 1984, new owners began pumping $7 million into C.B. in preparation for the park's 100th anniversary. Part of those funds would come from the sale of C.B.'s 1906 PTC carousel. This vintage ride—complete with two chariots, 23 horses, and 21 other animals including a camel, giraffe, lion, wolf, and a St. Bernard—was auctioned off piecemeal that December. Although it meant the loss of a splendid carousel, the revenues from the sale allowed the establishment of a new ferry service from Buffalo, the purchase of additional attractions, and a general refurbishment throughout the park. Perhaps a day late and a dollar short, though, Crystal Beach ceased operations after the 1989 season.

CRYSTAL BEACH, LAKE ERIE, ONTARIO, CANADA

Cystal Beach Cyclone and ballroom

Crystal Beach's rambling ballroom shares the limelight with the park's notorious Cyclone coaster circa 1929. AUTHOR'S COLLECTION

Giant Coaster's Art Deco station, Crystal Beach

The Giant Coaster's station in this 1984 scene was obviously newer than the 1916-built ride itself. This coaster was one of the last surviving side-friction rides. MIKE SCHAFER

Euclid Beach Park, Cleveland, Ohio

Euclid Beach Park, Cleveland, Ohio

This postcard from the 1930s was made when five of Euclid Beach's roller coasters existed at one time. AUTHOR'S COLLECTION

Euclid Beach Park entrance

For decades trolleys dropped off visitors at this entrance, which was built under one of the hills of the Thriller. JAMES P. MARCUS

Euclid Beach Park occupied 1,700 linear feet of sandy beach and 75 acres of wooded forest on the southern shore of Lake Erie, about eight miles from Cleveland's Public Square. Beginning in 1895, a local trolley line established service to the entrance gate, bringing bathers and picnickers even before the addition of varied entertainment attractions. Eventually, it was accessible from downtown by two streetcar lines and several passenger steamers plying Lake Erie. Founders aspired to make "Euclid Beach to Cleveland what Coney Island is to New York."

The park was originally managed by William R. Ryan Sr., a local businessman and politician also known as the father of Cleveland's summer resorts. Ryan patterned the park after its Eastern sister, offering a beer garden, freak shows, and gambling operations.

Dudley S. Humphrey II and six members of his family took over management of the park in 1901. After operating concessions at Euclid Beach, they had departed in 1899, dissatisfied with "gamblers, fakers, and questionable side shows." The Humphreys, previously known in Cleveland as candy and popcorn manufacturers, brought Euclid Beach into its glory years. Inventive and industrious, they made the park into a family entertainment center and implemented their own ingenuous ideas and high ideals, embodied in the slogan "Nothing to depress or demoralize." Finally, as an inducement to patrons, the Humphreys instituted a policy of "one fare, free gate, and no beer," charging only small fees for the attractions. This policy was maintained until the park closed in 1969.

The park was the scene of political gatherings, such as the local Democratic party "steer roast," and in 1910 the site of an important exhibition

40:—AERIAL VIEW OF EUCLID BEACH PARK, CLEVELAND. OHIO

The Bug, Euclid Beach

Like many traditional parks, Euclid Beach boasted a vintage Traver Engineering Tumble Bug ride, which Euclid simply called The Bug. Just beyond in this 1960s scene is another classic, the Flying Scooters. In the distant background a portion of the Flying Turns can be glimpsed. JAMES P. MARCUS

The Great American Racing Derby, Euclid Beach

One of Euclid's more unique rides was a sort of super merry-go-round known as the Great American Racing Derby. This high-powered ride simulated a high-speed horse race. In this scene, the steeds have become frozen in time. Euclid Beach has closed for the season. THE HUMPHREY COMPANY

flight by aviator Glen Curtis. And, of course, Euclid Beach had a wonderful array of rides. Among the most popular of early attractions was La Marcus Thompson's 1896 reprise of the 1884 Coney Island *Switch Back Railway*. It would lead to the construction of other coasters, including the *Scenic Railway* (1907), *Velvet Coaster* (1909; later known as *Aero Dips*), *Derby Racer* (1913; later known simply as the *Racing Coaster*), the *Thriller* (1924), and the *Flying Turns* (1930). Other rides over the years included a baroque-styled carousel, *The Bug* (a Traver Tumble bug), *Rocket Ships* (circle swing), *Mill Chute*, *Laff in the Dark*, the *Flying Ponies* (a very unusual tilted carousel with free-swinging suspended wooden horses), and the *Great American Racing Derby* mechanical horse race. Other facilities included the Log Cabin (the main pavilion), a lakefront pier and fountain, a maple-floored dance hall, and a skating rink complete with a rococo-styled Gavioli organ. Over 100 rides and concessions made Euclid Beach the epitome of amusement parks.

As the years passed, Euclid Beach Park changed: trolleys were replaced by buses and automobiles began to arrive more frequently. But attendance began to decline after World War II— slowly at first, and then with startling speed in the

1960s when changing lifestyles, lake pollution, rising operational costs, and racial incidents sent the once-loyal patrons to other diversions. The park closed forever on September 28, 1969.

Only the carved archway entrance, declared a historic Cleveland landmark in 1973, remains at the site as a memorial to past glories. Still, in 1985, Ohio created Euclid Beach State Park on the easternmost 16 acres of the old amusement park. Some vestige of the land's original purpose thus remains.

Idora Park, Youngstown, Ohio

Built by the Park & Falls Street Railway Company, Idora Park (originally called Terminal Park) opened officially on Decoration Day 1899. To draw passengers to the sparsely populated south side

Idora Park Wildcat

Idora. It seemed like such a peaceful park—until you stepped aboard the Wildcat. You were then aboard one of the most ferocious coasters of modern times. This view looks down the first drop and toward the far-end "fan curve" that cracked many a rib.

Idora Park in twilight

It was twilight at Idora Park in more ways than one when this scene was recorded on a warm summer evening in 1983. The end came in 1984. Things appear quiet at the Ferris wheel, but the Traver rocket ship ride is in full swing. Meanwhile, the Jack Rabbit coaster stays quietly hidden behind the trees.
MIKE SCHAFER

of Youngstown, they acquired a lease on seven acres next to Mill Creek Park. Like many electric railways of the time, the trolley wasn't built to get people to the park; the park was built to get people on the trolley cars.

Idora had a large bathhouse and a giant swimming pool connected to an underground salt-water spring, creating the only inland salt-water pool in the country. Because of a need for more space, the pool was filled in and the area converted to a kiddieland during the 1950s.

Although Idora did not have a wide array of coasters like some parks, its two surviving woodies were both winners in different ways. The oldest was the *Jack Rabbit*, built in 1910 as a side-friction coaster that was later converted to underfriction wheels. With larger but gentle, fun hills, the *Jack Rabbit* ("Back Wabbit" the year the park ran the trains backward) was a family favorite. The *Wildcat* was a PTC ride that went up

in 1929 and was ranked among the top ten roller coasters in the world.

In addition to the coasters, the park had a respectable collection of rides and attractions. One of the most famous was the *Old Mill*, later called *The Lost River*—a boat ride that took passengers through dark tunnels and ended with a thrilling drop. Idora also had a fun house, a haunted castle, a Ferris wheel, a *Tilt-A-Whirl*, and a circle swing.

A relentless recession, unfavorable weather, and persistent bad luck resulted in Idora going up for sale in 1982. In 1984, a welding accident caused a significant portion of the *Wildcat* to burn. The park operated that summer, but in the shadow of flourishing competitors like Cedar Point, Geauga Lake, and Kennywood—combined with the loss of the headlining *Wildcat*—the future was bleak. Add to that steel-mill closings in Youngstown that resulted in ever-declining attendance and you had one mighty bleak future.

When Idora Park closed for good at the end of the 1984 season, most rides were auctioned off. The coasters and many historic buildings were left behind as skeletal reminders.

Palisades Park, Fort Lee, New Jersey

Two hundred feet above the Hudson River lay an undeveloped tract of wooded palisades. While only a mile from Manhattan, inaccessibility kept the development that had been spilling out of New York City from reaching the cliffs until 1896. The Bergen County Traction Company built an electric railway that zigzagged up the cliffs in 1898, bringing passengers to a 38-acre picnic grove with a spectacular view of New York City.

By 1908, swings, horseback rides, a miniature train, and a carousel waited to entertain guests. Darts, a shooting gallery, and various ring games were also offered and spectators were treated to dirigible and balloon flights, high-diving horses, a circus, and Vaudeville acts. Later an aviary, farm, dance hall, and zoological gardens were among the attractions in the newly named Palisades Amusement Park.

The biggest "attraction" was advertised as the largest electric sign in the world: 400 feet long, with letters 18 feet high, 10,000 electric bulbs spelled out Palisades Amusement Park. At night it could be read from Long Island, 50 miles away and it surely attracted moths from as far away as New England.

By the end of the 1909 season, Palisades Park had become a full-fledged amusement park. Despite the successful season, investments had exceeded the financial means of the owners. So Nicholas and Joseph Schenck and Marcus Loew bought the park and added

PALISADES AMUSEMENT PARK, JERSEY CITY, N. J.

improvements like concrete sidewalks, a baby nursery, and a public address system called "Electric Enunciators."

The 1910 season heralded in three major new rides: an automobile race, the *Sleigh Ride* coaster, with sled-style cars, and the *Big Scenic* coaster, an electrified third-rail-powered coaster. In the 1920s, Palisades gained two more highly revered roller coasters. The *Skyrocket*, a John Miller creation, and one of Harry Traver's infamous *Cyclone* triplets; although that ride ran into a problem. Traver Engineering Company had assumed the land was level but later discovered a fairly extreme elevation variation, which required changes to the structure's height in places during construction. The resulting ride was extra rough and, never as popular as the *Skyrocket*, was removed in 1934. Shortly after, the *Skyrocket* was rebuilt and renamed *Cyclone*.

Jack and Irving Rosenthal had taken over the park by this time and had already survived their first big crisis. On July 2, 1932, some 10,000 park patrons witnessed the sky suddenly turn orange. When the smoke cleared, 19 people had been

Cyclone, Palisades Park

INSET: The centerpiece ride of Palisades was the Cyclone, heavily reconfigured by Joe McKee (of Philadelphia Toboggan Company fame) from the Skyrocket. AUTHOR'S COLLECTION

Midway, Palisades Park

Palisades Park, visible at night from Manhattan, was alive with lighting, as illustrated by this showpiece concession stand on the Midway. AUTHOR'S COLLECTION

The Pike, Long Beach, California

An aerial of The Pike at Long Beach in 1955 reveals the park in the automobile age—nearly half the land is now devoted to parking space even though the Pacific Electric interurban was still serving the area at the time. Dominant in the scene is the renown Cyclone Racer coaster, one of the finest roller coasters ever built; nearby is a National Amusement Devices junior coaster. Additional attractions were located in the buildings on the fringe of the park itself. AUTHOR'S COLLECTION

injured and about an eighth of the park was a smoldering ruin. The Creation exhibit, *Old Mill*, shooting gallery, *Whip*, and *Motor Parkway* were gone. The fire wasn't out until six o'clock that evening, but the Rosenthals, ever the showmen, reopened later that same night.

In 1937, Palisades unveiled what some regulars considered to be the the park's most frightening roller coaster, the *Lake Placid Bobsled*. A member of the *Flying Turns* genre of coaster in which bobsled-type cars on rubber caster wheels

careened down a wood-trough track, *Lake Placid Bobsled* trains had to be re-engineered to keep them from somersaulting!

In August 1944, the Palisades again found itself fighting for its life. A fire had broken out on the *Virginia Reel*, and when it was over, the carousel, a small *Scenic Railway*, the fun house, *Glass House*, dance pavilion, and most of the midway and *Skyrocket* roller coaster were destroyed. Nearly half of the 200 parked cars were devoured as gas tanks exploded and tires melted.

A renovated park opened in 1945 with cinder block buildings and a host of new rides, including a 64-horse carousel supplied by the Philadelphia Toboggan Company. As with other traditional parks of the era, Palisades battled TV and other new postwar diversions, and even gained a bit of claim to fame in the 1962 Freddy Cannon hit, "Down at Palisades Park." It remained a well-maintained park through its last year of operation, 1971, when it was sold to a Texas-based development corporation, rezoned, demolished, and replaced by bland apartment buildings.

The Pike, Long Beach, California

On the south side of Los Angeles, some 30 miles down the shore from the parks of Venice and Santa Monica (Chapter 3), Long Beach was once home to another popular seaside amusement area known throughout most of its history as The Pike. Beginning in 1902, amusement rides and attractions lined the beach and a pier on the surf side of this major Los Angeles satellite city. For years, the dominating ride was the looming *Cyclone Racer* roller coaster, considered one of the all-time best coasters ever built. As with other L.A.-area amusement parks, The Pike served in several Hollywood movies and TV sitcoms (the *Cyclone Racer* makes cameo appearances in the 1953 sci-fi classic *The Beast From 20,000 Fathoms;* and in an episode of the 1950s/1960s TV series "Leave It To Beaver," the Beav, big brother Wally, and green-at-the-gills Eddie Haskell take a spin on the famous racing coaster).

In 1949, the park was updated to become the Nu-Pike, but changing times and attitudes of the postwar period rendered the park as a perceived nuisance to city fathers, who wanted to improve Long Beach's image. In doing so, the *Cyclone Racer* was razed to make way for the retired *Queen Mary* ocean liner; already the park had been renamed Queens Park. The last of the amusement area was closed in 1979.

Riverview Park, Chicago

Like the Cubs' Wrigley Field, Marshall Field's department store, and the Museum of Science and Industry, Riverview Park was a Chicago institution. Initially a private picnic ground, the wooded park was opened to the public in 1903 as Sharpshooters Park, so-named because of its early years as a private firing range. As a public facility, the park, which sat along the North Branch of the Chicago River, was renamed Riverview Sharpshooters Park.

The owners wasted no time in adding amusements for the 1904 season, including the first of many roller coasters, a Figure 8 ride known as the *White Flyer*. Other attractions included a water ride, the *Temple of Mirth* fun house, and a midway. In 1906 the park expanded by 50 acres and a half million dollars of new attractions were added, including a primitive forerunner of today's virtual-reality dark rides in which patrons rode railcars through a darkened building while view-

ing movies of exotic foreign locations projected outside the car windows.

The year 1907 brought yet another increase in size and the number of attractions, and the place became known simply as Riverview Park. That year, two of the park's landmarks also opened: the new twin-towered front gate and the *Shoot-the-Chutes* ride. Both would welcome visitors for the next 60 years. The $50,000, 4,700-foot-run *Velvet Coaster* also opened in 1907, as did a water carousel known as the *Aquarasel*.

During the ensuing years, new rides and attractions mushroomed as did attendance. One of the most elaborate attractions (with a price tag of nearly a quarter million dollars) was the *Battle of the Monitor and Merrimac*, opened in 1908. Situated in a large, turreted building, it presented a remake of the historic Civil War battle of the two

Main entrance, Riverview Park, Chicago

Festooned with incandescent bulbs, the twin-towered portal through which millions of visitors passed to enter Chicago's Riverview Park was a landmark on "the longest street in America," Western Avenue. Shown circa late 1940s, the ornate gateway was unveiled in 1907 and remained to the end of the park's life 60 years later. The coaster at far right was the Flash (a.k.a., Silver Flash and Pippin) built in 1920; the one seen through the gate in the distance is the Blue Streak (formerly the Skyrocket), which in 1959 was rebuilt into the ferocious Fireball. AUTHOR'S COLLECTION

Riverview Park, Chicago, circa 1915

A westerly view from Riverview's cleverly named "Eye-Full Tower" reveals the park's wide array of attractions. The building in the lower left corner of the photo houses a freak show; the round building at upper left housed the Sinking of the Titanic attraction and is surrounded in part by the original Blue Streak coaster (two coasters at Riverview carried this name), in part occupying the future site of the Bobs. At top center in the distance is the lift hill for the Shoot-the-Chutes and to the right the Velvet Coaster; to the left of the Chutes is the carousel building. In the lower right corner of the photo is the Gee Whiz coaster, later named Greyhound. COURTESY DEREK GEE AND RALPH LOPEZ, SHARPSHOOTERS PRODUCTIONS

famous boats. This was also the year Riverview took delivery of PTC No. 17 for $18,000—at that time one of the most ornate carousels ever built.

Located on Chicago's near northwest side, the park grew to over 100 acres, encompassing the northwest quadrant of Western Avenue and Belmont. Being on major streetcar and bus routes gave the park easy access for Chicagoans.

By the 1910s, Riverview had already gained a reputation as a "coaster park," sporting seven coasters at the start of the 1910 season. By the early 1920s, the park boasted nine coasters, some having already replaced earlier coasters. In 1924, the park built its 15th—and by far its most famous—coaster, the *Bobs*. This Prior & Church ride would reign over all other Midwest coasters until closing day 1967, and to this day its name is mentioned in hushed, reverent whispers.

There was some rough sailing for Riverview during the Depression, especially considering that it also had to compete with the Century of Progress exhibition in Chicago in 1933 and 1934. Riverview touted its "Century of Nonsense" pageant, a parody of the nearby world's fair and cut gate admission drastically to two cents on selected days, which boosted attendance. Good things came out of the Depression, though, including three attractions that would remain with the park to the end: the *Aladdin's Castle* fun house, the unique *Flying Turns* coaster (purchased from the Century of Progress), and the *Pair-O-Chutes* parachute jump (built from the Eye-Full Tower).

Riverview did well during the World War II years, since gas rationing kept Chicagoans on the home front. Riverview was a cheap streetcar or trolley bus ride away. However, once the war was over, the park began to experience a disturbing decline in attendance for the first time in its history as Americans took to the highways in ever-increasing numbers—or they began staying home evenings to partake in a new national "fad": television. To stem the tide, the park continued to add new rides and remodel. In 1959, the park rebuilt its John Miller-designed *Blue Streak* coaster into the high-speed *Fireball*.

Heavy promotion throughout Mid-America in the postwar period made Riverview legendary, and it became a popular destination for church groups or kids on school outings from cities all over the Midwest. The future looked bright enough that the park spent over $300,000 to have the Philadelphia Toboggan Company build the new *Jetstream* roller coaster for the 1965 season. It would be Riverview's last new ride.

In 1967, after two years of renovation, elderly PTC carousel No. 17 was rededicated. Park-goers continued to flow in, urged by ads in the *Chicago Tribune* to experience the "90-MPH" *Bobs* and "100-MPH" *Fireball* (greatly exaggerating their speeds) as well as by radio spots by park spokesman Dick "Two Ton" Baker. At the end of the 1967 season, the park closed and a huge sign at the main entrance announced the start date of Riverview's 1968 season. . . but suddenly word spread that the park had closed for good.

Chicagoans were outraged, and letters and editorials appeared in newspapers throughout the Chicagoland area. There was a call to reopen the park for a day so everyone could have one last visit—which undoubtedly would not have worked if only because Riverview would have been gridlocked with people saying their final good-byes. Instead, the rides—including the park's seven roller coasters—were auctioned off, and those not purchased were demolished.

The reasons for the closing remained shrouded in rumor, ranging from racial tension to undertable political dealings orchestrated by then Chicago Mayor Richard J. Daley. The most plausible reason was probably economical: Although Riverview was making money in the end, the value of the land on which it sat had risen significantly after the war, and offers from developers had increased markedly. Everybody has a price, they say, and that of Riverview's owners had apparently been met.

Marine Causeway, Riverview Park

In a 1920s-era view that looks southward from atop the lift hill of the Shoot-the-Chutes, the jewel of a building that houses PTC carousel No. 17 stands prominent. The wide walkway to the right was known as the Marine Causeway on account of its proximity to the North Branch Chicago River (mostly obscured by a row of trees). In the distance is the new Bobs roller coaster, completed in 1924. COURTESY DEREK GEE AND RALPH LOPEZ, SHARPSHOOTERS PRODUCTIONS

Puzzletown, Riverview Park

Riverview was chock full of various shows, walk-throughs, and other odd-ball attractions, such as Puzzletown, shown in 1921. COURTESY DEREK GEE AND RALPH LOPEZ, SHARPSHOOTERS PRODUCTIONS

Lakeside Park, Denver, Colorado

Even in the new millennium, it's possible to experience an amusement park of the 1940s, and Denver's Lakeside Park is just the place. Filled with Art Deco architecture, neon lighting, wonderful rides, and beautiful landscaping, Lakeside is an instant trip into the Big Band era. MIKE SCHAFER

Camden Park, Huntington, West Virginia

Tucked away in a wooded area along the Ohio River is little Camden Park, just one of numerous traditional parks that have managed to flourish into the theme park era. OTTO P. DOBNICK

SURVIVORS
The Traditional Park Lives

A look at a sampling of classics from the past that are looking to the future

The traditional amusement park concept is still alive in America, although it may be somewhat threatened by the monstrous commercial theme parks. Still, there are many, many loyal enthusiasts who prefer to catch a glimpse of history in a 50-, 60-, or 70-year-old park rather be bombarded by an onslaught of television and/or movie characters. Most of these parks have sought to maintain their natural settings and some of their original structures and attractions while keeping apace with modern developments where rides are concerned. The result can be a delightful combination of those "old-fashioned" park concepts (like a simple carousel and a swim) and the advantages of modern amusement park technology and engineering (the hypercoasters!).

Numerous North American traditional parks of varying sizes—some of them dating from the nineteenth century—have survived into the new millennium in America. A few have been "theme park-ized" to one degree or another, but most, in some way, retain their "good ole days" charm and nostalgia—and judging by attendance, many folks still like that. Here is a sampling of "survivors."

Cyclone Racer, Ferris Wheel and Miniature Merry-Go-Round, Cedar Point, on Lake Erie

Cedar Point, circa 1940

Guarding the lakefront, the Cyclone (misidentified as the Cyclone Racer on this postcard) lords over the crowds at Cedar Point's beach. World War II devastated the park in terms of patronage and the ability to maintain the premises. The Cyclone was in such need of repair after the war, that it was deemed a loss and torn down early in the 1950s. AUTHOR'S COLLECTION

Cedar Point, Sandusky, Ohio

Of all the traditional amusement parks that have survived the century, none are more successful than Cedar Point. From a resort that was failing by 1950, it has grown into a destination park that ranks in the top ten in America, among both theme and traditional parks combined. In addition, Cedar Fair, Ltd., the corporation behind the name, has acquired Valley Fair in Shakopee, Minnesota, Dorney Park in Allentown, Pennsylvania, Worlds of Fun in Kansas City, Missouri, and Knott's Berry Farm in Buena Park, California.

Cedar Point's history as an amusement resort began in 1870 when a German cabinetmaker

from Sandusky opened a small beer garden, dance floor, bathhouse, and children's playground on the Cedar Point peninsula (which is more an island than a peninsula) jutting north into Lake Erie. Louis Zistel's enterprise was short-lived, closing that same summer.

By the 1880s, though, sailing and bathing parties to the Point had become the rage, and two Sandusky businessmen realized the commercial potential of Cedar Point. The attractions were still bathing, fishing, and picnicking, but as many as a thousand people visited each day—not only for the facilities, but also the pleasant steamboat ride between the mainland and the park.

In 1887, the Cedar Point Pleasure Resort Company was formed, and the development of Cedar Point as a major resort began in earnest. The 1888 season opened with the new, sprawling Grand Pavilion, containing a large theater and concert hall, an observation tower, photo studio, bowling alleys, saloon, and kitchen. A shooting gallery, merry-go-round, baseball, football, lawn tennis, boat rentals, and the natural beauty of the Point also beckoned.

By 1890, Cedar Point was referred to as the "Coney Island of the West." The first of a multitude of roller coasters that would inhabit Cedar Point arrived in 1892: La Marcus Thompson's sensational *Switchback Railway*. Daily crowds now sometimes exceeded 6,000, but competition for neighboring resorts began cutting into Cedar Point's popularity. Something needed to change.

Change came in late 1897 in the form of Indiana businessman George A. Boeckling. By opening day 1898, an updated, refurbished, and repainted Cedar Point was awaiting patrons. When the season closed, modest gains had been made, and Boeckling, the master showman, declared Cedar Point "Ohio's Greatest Pleasure Resort" in widely distributed brochures. Hotels were built to accommodate long-term guests.

In 1902 the 46-foot-high *Racer* coaster, built by Fred Ingersoll, debuted, joined by a fun house, a miniature steam railroad, and a pony track. Still, there was no delineated amusement area. After Boeckling visited the St. Louis World's Fair in 1904, the "landscape" of Cedar Point began to change dramatically. At the fair, Boeckling was impressed not only by such ride devices as the Ferris wheel and Thompson's *Scenic Railway*, but also by the fair's impressive architecture and design. Boeckling's trip signaled the start of Cedar Point's golden age—an age that opened in

1906 with the new, 600-room Breakers Hotel and a defined amusement area known as Amusement Circle. By this time, construction had started on a huge new entertainment complex, the Coliseum.

Still newer amusement attractions included a circle swing, another carousel, Hales's Tours, fun houses, bowling alleys, a penny arcade, and Mundy's Coney Island Wild Animal Show. The popularity of the Amusement Circle required continual addition and updating of attractions. Roller coaster technology was rapidly changing, and in 1908 the *Dip the Dips Scenic Railway* was added. Four years later, Erwin Vettel built the faster *Leap the Dips*, and a few years later the new *Leap Frog Scenic Railway* replaced the *Dip the Dips*.

Boeckling was on the cutting edge of motion-picture exhibition at Cedar Point when he displayed Edison's *The Great Train Robbery*. A young resort employee by the name of Sam Warner was so impressed with this new entertainment that he and his brother Albert purchased a print of Edison's film and set out through the Midwest to show it. It's doubtful that Boeckling realized he had spawned not only one of America's great movie studios, but what was to become Cedar Point's largest competitor—today's Time Warner, one-time owner of the Six Flags empire.

By the 1920s, Cedar Point was a well established resort, with people arriving at the park from all over the Midwest via rail (with a ferry connection from Sandusky to the park itself) and by Great Lakes steamboats from as far away as Detroit, Toledo, and Cleveland. In 1915, however, the first road was built into the park, and on July 4, 1915, some 3,000 people arrived by automobile.

During the Roaring Twenties, the Amusement Circle continued to be updated. Kiddieland, *Noah's Ark*, a *Shoot-the-Chutes*, *Bluebeard's Palace*, and a *Tilt-A-Whirl* were added, and in 1929, the *Racer* roller coaster was replaced with the Fred Church-designed *Cyclone* coaster, described as frightening, awesome, bone-jarring

Cedar Point in the 1990s

A half century after World War II finds a vibrant, sprawling Cedar Point resort and amusement complex encompassing the entire peninsula. The famed Hotel Breakers—expanded from its original size—stands bright and clean, and quite convenient to park attractions. In the background are the Mean Streak, Gemini, and Magnum XL-200 coasters. COURTESY CEDAR POINT

and—one of the finest roller coasters ever constructed in the Midwest.

Boeckling—the man behind Cedar Point's success—died in 1931, right as the Depression took a stranglehold on the industry. Cedar Point creaked and groaned under the economics of the Great Depression, but the repeal of Prohibition, an increase in convention business, and the era of Big Band dancing—helped keep the park afloat.

Alas, World War II put another crimp on growth, and Cedar Point emerged from the war era in deplorable condition and on the verge of bankruptcy. The park was leased to new operators, and improvements soon began to surface. The Breakers Hotel was modernized and refurbished, and the concessionaires in the Amusement Circle began to overhaul and spruce up their rides and games. One major loss was the *Cyclone*, which had to be torn down due to years of neglect.

In 1957, a causeway was opened, providing auto traffic with a shortcut to the park from Sandusky and further increasing traffic. Control of the park by this time had come under developer George Roose, who initially had announced plans to raze the park and put up housing. Public outcry had been so vocal that the governor of Ohio intervened. Roose saw the error of his ways and soon announced new plans to develop Cedar Point into the "Disneyland of the Midwest." As the rebuilding of Cedar Point took place, management strove to find both unique, old rides to refurbish, and one-of-a-kind new rides and attractions to add to the mix, including a suspended monorail. Attendance and profits increased, and so did the crescendo of improvements.

Ever more spectacular rides and attractions—notably the Cedar Point & Lake Erie Railroad, the *Mill Race* log-flume ride, and the *Sky Ride*—were added, further increasing attendance. Finally,

Cedar Point—which had been coasterless (save for a *Wild Mouse*) since the razing of the *Cyclone*—received a large new wood coaster, the *Blue Streak*, in 1964. Thus began Cedar Point's rebirth as a coaster mecca. Heavy park promotion and a whole new range of major coasters took Cedar Point to new heights: the *Cedar Creek Mine Ride* (1969), the *Corkscrew* (1976), the massive *Gemini* racing coaster (1978), *Junior Gemini* (1979), *Disaster Transport* (1985), *Iron Dragon* (1987), and the new king of the park, *Magnum XL-200*, in 1989. *Magnum* was at the time the tallest coaster in the world. The first major wood-track coaster since the *Blue Streak* followed in 1991 when the *Mean Streak* was launched; then came *Raptor* (1994), *Mantis* (1996), and then the ultimate—*Millennium Force* (2000), the world's tallest and fastest coaster. Cedar Point can only go up (and down and up again) from here.

Conneaut Lake Park, Pennsylvania

Conneaut Lake Park is a wonderful lakeside park located in northwestern Pennsylvania near the town of Conneaut Lake as well as Meadeville. The park dates back to 1892 when it opened as an exposition park, fostered in part by the Pittsburgh, Shenango & Lake Erie Railroad (today's Bessemer & Lake Erie) and a visionary named Frank Mantor. For the subsequent 100-plus years, the park has maintained much of its original charm. The traditional style of many of the park buildings, the midway, the beach, cottages and the rambling Conneaut Hotel (opened in 1903) give the park an old-time ambiance. Adding to this are several municipal streets which criss-cross the park grounds, though some have been closed off with the gating of the park in 1990.

Dreamland Ballroom, Conneaut Lake Park

Opened in 1909, Conneaut's Dreamland Ballroom, shown in the summer of 1994, occupies a city block and is still used for dancing and other group functions. The main level houses concessions. MIKE SCHAFER

The size of the park and the number of its attractions have fluctuated at times over the years, as it has been difficult to attract the large crowds necessary to capitalize new endeavors. The park's location is relatively remote—which is part of its charm but also a liability, as Conneaut Lake serves a modestly populated area; the nearest large city is Erie, Pennsylvania, about 30 miles north—and Erie has its own traditional park, Waldameer. Competition from Six Flags Ohio (Geauga Lake) and Kennywood, both less than three hours away, probably hasn't helped.

Though not known as a "coaster park," Conneaut nonetheless is home to one of the best old woodies around, the venerable *Blue Streak*, tucked away in the woods but only a couple minutes' walk from the Hotel Conneaut and nearby motels. This is a must ride for coaster fans.

The park is also home to the country's oldest *Tumble Bug* ride which is located along the Midway. A beautiful carousel built by D. C. Muller & Bros. in 1905 (with some updated carvings done

Blue Streak, Conneaut Lake Park

Hidden in the woods at serene Conneaut Lake Park is a raucous, rip-roarin' roller coaster that is a perennial favorite of coaster fanatics everywhere. Designed by Ed Vettel Sr., the Blue Streak opened in 1937. The ride begins with a trip through "Skunk Tunnel" (you can guess why it got that name), and the first two steep drops are borderline unbelievable in terms of their punch, especially from the back seat. Vintage NAD trains with operating headlights make this an all-time classic, shown here careening through the woods in 1979. MIKE SCHAFER

Dorney Park, Allentown, Pennsylvania

This folder from late in Dorney's classic era, prior to the park's massive revamping and expansion beginning in the late 1980s, shows the park grounds when they were still ungated, and public roads passed through the park. Prominent in the scene is the Coaster, which is surrounded by picnic groves. Today's massive Steel Force hypercoaster stands alongside the venerable 1923 woodie. AUTHOR'S COLLECTION

by Carousel Works of Mansfield, Ohio) lives next door to the *Blue Streak*. Wrapped around the base of the *Blue Streak* is a miniature railroad. Other rides include a *Tilt-A-Whirl*, Ferris wheel, *Scrambler*, *Paratrooper*, and *Whip*. For the toddlers, a Kiddieland stands at the site of the now-abandoned railroad terminal.

Conneaut Lake Park also offers Cliffhanger Falls, a water-slide complex that includes Otter Creek Adventure River. The soft sandy beach that rests along the crystal-clear shoreline of Conneaut Lake offers the simple pleasures of

ALLENTOWN, PENNSYLVANIA

Dorney Park

"One of America's Greatest Amusement Parks"

swimming relaxation, and the adjacent Beach House building houses a popular pub. Full meals can be had in the elegant dining room of the Hotel Conneaut, whose huge, rocking-chair-equipped porch offers a serene view of the lake.

Dorney Park, Allentown, Pennsylvania

Nestled in the rolling hills of southeastern Pennsylvania just west of Allentown/Bethlehem, Dorney Park oddly enough began as a trout hatchery during the Civil War era. It grew into a recreational gathering spot popular with churches and fraternal groups, with a zoo and games such as croquet and ten pins as the main attractions. As the nineteenth century wound down, the arrival of a trolley line made the park exceptionally accessible to folks in the Lehigh Valley. Rides and attractions were introduced during this period, including a *Scenic Railway*, *Circle Swing*, and the *Cave of the Winds*, presumably an early dark ride or walk-through attraction.

From this modest beginning grew one of the East's most well-known and loved traditional amusement parks, loaded with some classic rides, including a Dentzel carousel, the *Rockets* (a Traver *Circle Swing*), the *Cuddle-Up* (a fascinating, mechanically complex spinning ride, later enclosed and renamed *Iceberg*), *Scooter* (one of the best bumper car rides to survive into the 1980s), the *Journey to the Center of the Earth* dark ride, the *Indy 500* (electric car racing ride) and the *Dorney Park Zephyr* miniature train. The centerpiece ride for many years was the *Coaster*, a 1923 product of the Philadelphia Toboggan Company. Modified with a new, deviously twisted track layout in 1930, the *Coaster* in 1989 finally received a real name: *Thunderhawk*.

The late 1980s and the 1990s saw vast changes for Dorney when it was acquired by Cedar Fair, Ltd., of Cedar Point fame. One of the most significant early changes was the addition of a new wood coaster, the 4,000-foot-run *Hercules*, with an amazing 157-foot drop off a bluff to the surface of Lake Dorney. Another welcomed addition was a new water park known as Wildwater Kingdom and, for the little kids, Camp Snoopy kiddieland.

Today's ride lineup includes some of the old favorites such as the Dentzel carousel, *Thunderhawk*, miniature railroad, and the *Whip* (dating from 1920, this might be the oldest ride on the property), as well as new rides: the *Dominator* (an extreme open-elevator ride); *Thunder Creek*

Mountain flume ride; *Thunder Creek Canyon* whitewater rapids ride. Several new coasters have joined the 1989 *Hercules*, including the *Laser; Dragon Coaster* (no relation to the ride of the same name at Playland, Rye, New York); a modern *Wild Mouse*; the mile-long-plus, 75-MPH *Steel Force* (1997); and, for 2001, the *Talon*—Dorney's first inverted coaster.

Unfortunately, several of the colorful, classic old buildings, rides, attractions, and lighting were removed in the multi-year makeover, and Dorney's brightly colored "circus" look (including the fondly remembered Alfundo the Clown park mascot) has given way to the monochrome colors and decor typical of today's theme parks. But, at the expense of some its old-time charm, Dorney now has more rides and attractions than ever, and the attendance figures reflect that.

Elitch Gardens, Denver, Colorado

In the late 1880s, a young couple named Mary and John Elitch, owners of a downtown Denver restaurant, bought 16 acres of farmland at what is now 38th Avenue and Tennyson Street. They intended to raise vegetables for their restaurant, but, inspired by the Woodward Gardens in San Francisco, John and Mary instead decided to create a zoological garden and summer theater on their new land. Opening day was May 1, 1890, and Denverites arrived by the thousands, joined by such international celebrities as P. T. Barnum and Mr. and Mrs. Tom Thumb of circus fame. Thus the renowned Elitch's Zoological Gardens, as "America's Garden of Fun" had its beginning. Famed Elitch Theater opened the following year.

Dorney Park entrance

For years, visitors arriving through Dorney's north gate were greeted by the huge countenance of the park's mascot, Alfundo the Clown. The juggling jester sat atop a "stage" whose marquee featured the park name in incandescent lights—all of which sat above a cleverly designed building that served as an entrance to both the Scooter (bumper cars) ride and the Coaster. This was amusement park art and architecture at its classic best, but it became a victim of the times, and Alfundo himself was last seen at the Allentown unemployment office, in line with former workers of Bethlehem Steel. OTTO P. DOBNICK

Six Flags Elitch Gardens, Denver, Colorado

You're getting an eagle's-eye view of the new Elitch Gardens, relocated to larger quarters near downtown Denver in 1995 after more than a century of being located in a residential neighborhood in northwest Denver. The new location allowed for a waterpark (lower right) and a new amphitheater for concerts—a popular venue at the new Elitch's. Lording over the park at the far end in this 2000 scene is the Twister II coaster.

Tragedy struck in 1892 when John Elitch died, leaving the park to his wife. Mary soldiered on, however, and nurtured the park into stardom. After a visit to Coney Island's Luna Park in 1904, she was inspired to add mechanical rides to her park, and among the first was a Figure-8 coaster; a Philadelphia Toboggan Company carousel followed in 1905. More rides followed, and in the Roaring Twenties a dance hall debuted.

From the 1920s through 1975, the Trocadero Ballroom reigned as the "Summer Home of America's Biggest Bands." It was built at the time big-name bands were getting their start, and the succession of famous names who played there—the Dorseys, Les Brown, Ozzie Nelson, Lawrence Welk, Guy Lombardo—rivaled the roster of theatrical greats that appeared at Elitch Theater, among them Cecil B. DeMille, Harold Lloyd, Edward G. Robinson, and Gloria Swanson.

Meanwhile, the park—now known as Elitch Gardens or simply Elitch's—continued to introduce new amusement rides and attractions, including a major new PTC roller coaster, the *Skyrocket* (later renamed *Wildcat*), in 1926 and a new PTC carousel in 1928. Meanwhile, the park continued to maintain an array of award-winning floral gardens, as befitting its name.

For the 1964 season, Elitch's debuted its *Mister Twister* wood coaster, designed by PTC's John Allen. The slow, short, unexciting ride was a bust, and the park had Allen come back to rework and enlarge it. The result was a masterpiece of coaster thrills that became a Denver institution—like Elitch's itself—and achieved a "top three" rating.

Interest in ballroom dancing was on the decline by the 1970s and at the close of the 1975 season the Trocadero ballroom was taken down to make way for the Theatre Plaza—the initial phase of a five-year improvement campaign.

Elitch's was dogged by one major problem: space. Confined by the surrounding residential neighborhood (interestingly, within walking distance of rival Lakeside Park), there was little room to expand, and in 1995 Elitch's relocated to larger quarters near downtown. Unfortunately, the outrageous *Twister* and beloved *Wildcat* were orphaned and leveled. A brand-new woodie, *Twister II*, would reign over the new Elitch Gardens along with a larger-than-ever selection of rides, including several steel coasters. In 1997, Elitch's was acquired by Premier Parks and in 1999 was renamed Six Flags Elitch Gardens, maintaining a name rooted in Denver history for more than a century.

Kennywood Park, West Mifflin, Pennsylvania

Our story of Kennywood Park opens in the mid 1800s ...

Once upon a time, in the 1860s, 12 miles outside Pittsburgh, on a bluff high above the Monongahela River, lived a coal mining family named Kenny. Old Man Kenny had a farm (E-I-E-I-O), and on his farm he had a picnic spot that became known as Kenny's Grove. One day in 1898, the big, bad Monongahela Street Railway Company came to grandpa's house and said "My what a big picnic grove you have." "The better to lease you," said Anthony Kenny. So in 1898 the trolley company opened Kennywood Park on the farm it leased from Kenny, and we all played happily ever after.

This little ditty pretty well sums up the launching of what today is considered by many park historians to be the best traditional amusement park in America. Kennywood is not the biggest traditional park nor does it have the most coasters (those two claims go to Cedar Point), but Kennywood has excelled above all others in preserving the look and feel of a traditional early twentieth century amusement park.

In an effort to preserve the park's rustic beauty, Kennywood's original structures—among them the dance pavilion, casino (restaurant), and Carousel building—were strategically placed in open-air fashion throughout the park, separated by gardens, walkways, and picnic areas, all encompassing a lagoon. The dance hall only lasted 76 years as a result of fire, but the casino and carousel buildings are still in use more than a century after their construction. The open areas between these key buildings have accommodated an amazing

Kennywood Park, West Mifflin, Pennsylvania

Lots of things have changed at Kennywood, the queen of traditional parks. And lots of things haven't. Some of the buildings, such as this housing a concession stand, date back more than 100 years. This is just one of numerous reasons this stellar park near Pittsburgh calls itself "America's Finest Traditional Amusement Park" MIKE SCHAFER

Kennywood Park Midway, 1920s

Kennywood in the Roaring Twenties was as much a delight then as now. Prominent in this scene from about the time of the opening of the Pippin coaster in 1924 is the Bug House (note the backward sign). Over the years it was re-themed and carried other names as well. At right is a classic Traver circle swing, which at this time was known as the Seaplane. COURTESY KENNYWOOD PARK

Kennywood Park, 1980s

A sudden shower has temporarily cleared Kennywood's midway on a summer evening in 1980. A combination of Art Deco and "mod" architecture makes for a dazzling, magical night environment throughout the park. MIKE SCHAFER

variety of new rides and attractions as the park grew. Boating on the lake was a first-year attraction, and Kennywood's first mechanical ride at about the same time was a Dentzel carousel. The *Old Mill* ride opened in 1901 and celebrated its 100th anniversary in 2001. Like many other parks, Kennywood's first coaster, in 1902, was an Ingersoll Figure-8 ride, the *Toboggan*, followed by the *Scenic Railway* in 1903. By this time, Kennywood also featured a Steeplechase horse-racing ride, fun house, Ferris wheel, and miniature railway as well as vaudeville shows, live bands, shooting ranges, and bowling. Park managers knew early on that accommodating picnic groups would be key to Kennywood's success, and to this day picnicking remains a Pittsburgh-area ritual for all manner of groups and company picnics.

In 1906 the railway sold Kennywood to the Henninger and McSwigan families, who run the park to this day. Thus began an ongoing, aggressive campaign to add new rides and attractions (and yet keep popular older ones) to keep patrons coming back for more, and the first such major new ride was the *Aerial Racer* racing coaster, opening in 1910 to rave reviews. In 1911, the *Speed-O-Plane* coaster opened as "the longest and fastest ride in the country."

The 1920s were a golden age for Kennywood, with many developments and rides that still exist at the park. The decade started with the new *Jack Rabbit* "ravine" coaster (using the surrounding terrain to enhance its thrills), which quickly rose to being "the most popular attraction between New York and Chicago." Then came the *Pippin* in 1924, a coaster destined to be central to Kennywood's esteemed reputation in the coming years. In 1927, the new *Racer* replaced the old coaster of the same name. The Roaring Twenties also saw the addition of *Dodgem* bumper cars, a 16-car *Whip*, Traver Engineering *Tumble-Bug* (today's *Turtle* ride), Ferris wheel, an electric miniature railroad by Dayton Fun House, and the *Seaplane* (Traver circle swing). Older rides were remodeled. In 1925, on the site of today's new Lost Kennywood, the park opened a huge combination swimming pool and grandstand.

Kennywood weathered the Depression better than most parks, but survival did not come easily. Attendance dropped over 60 percent by 1933 and growth, in terms of new rides and attractions, was almost nil, with one notable exception: the *Noah's Ark* walk-through, which has since become a symbol of Kennywood. By the late 1930s, Kennywood had entered the Big Band era, and the Dance Pavilion underwent an Art Deco makeover. In fact, the popular Art Deco look began to spread to other selected rides and attractions.

World War II ushered in a whole new set of problems, mainly shortages of materials and manpower and the rationing of gasoline and. . . whiskey. Nonetheless, Kennywood became a welcome respite for soldiers on leave and war-weary civilians seeking relief from depressing news; the park gave out more than 2 million complementary tickets to service personnel. After the war, Kennywood began a major revamping of the grounds and the rides, along with some new ride installations. Of particular importance was the enlargement of the Kiddieland section—complete with the

new *Little Dipper* junior wood coaster—to accommodate postwar baby boomers.

The 1950s roared in with all sorts of changes. Television became the nemesis of many a park, but Kennywood used it to its advantage by heavily promoting the park on local TV with nationally known TV personalities like the Lone Ranger, Captain Kangaroo, and Clarabell the Clown from the wildly popular Howdy Doody Show. Customers flooded into the park. New rides for the decade included the *Rotor*, *Wild Mouse* coaster, *Octopus*, and *Scrambler*.

The 1960s were a period of doubt, as traditional parks from coast to coast began to falter. For Kennywood, though, it was largely business as usual—with one major exception: the rebuilding of the *Pippin* coaster. Park mechanical supervisor Andrew Vettel completely redesigned and rebuilt the ride following the 1967 season, keeping the

Kennywood's Thunderbolt

Kennywood's signature ride, the revered Thunderbolt, has two birthdays, 1924 and 1968. It is the result of what happens if you cross a 1924-built ravine coaster designed by John Miller with a 1968-built new section of trackage and hills designed by Andrew Vettel. The Thunderbolt is one of the very few coasters in North America whose final drop is, at 90 feet, its longest. In this 1980 scene, one of the Thunderbolt's nifty NAD (National Amusement Devices) 1958-era trains is circling through the new section of trackage before the two last drops. And the "T-Bolt," we assure you, is good to the last drop. MIKE SCHAFER

Lost Kennywood

In a stroke of brilliance in part designed to cater to patrons whose median age was increasing, Kennywood in 1998 transformed what had been a parking lot (and, earlier, the swimming pool and before that the Speed-O-Plane coaster) into a whole new sub-park dubbed Lost Kennywood. Complete with a classic Shoot-the-Chutes (one of whose boats has just created quite a splash in this scene), the new area exudes the tranquility of early twentieth century parks. COURTESY KENNYWOOD PARK

ravine section and melding it to a new ground-level rotary of hills and trackage. In 1968, a legend was unveiled: the incomparable *Thunderbolt*. With the nationwide coaster revival of the 1970s came the *Thunderbolt*'s "discovery" outside the realm of Pittsburgh, and it was spotlighted in the *New York Times* as the Number One roller coaster in the world. Also with the 1970s came pay-one-price fees—and Kennywood's worst fire, in 1975, destroying several rides and attractions. Nonetheless, the park embarked on one of its largest expansion and rehab programs ever as the 1970s played out, including new land purchases.

By the 1980s, the amusement park industry was booming, particularly in the realm of theme parks, but Kennywood enjoyed new prominence as the self-proclaimed "Roller Coaster Capital of the World." And 1980 brought the park's first new coaster since 1968, the steel-track *Laser Loop*. Hundreds of members of the new American Coaster Enthusiasts group descended on the park to dedicate the new ride and launch a new era of public awareness about roller coasters and traditional amusement parks in general, and Kennywood in

particular. In 1987, Kennywood achieved National Historic Landmark status.

In 1991, Kennywood introduced its towering *Steel Phantom* steel-track looping coaster, whose record-breaking 225-foot second drop dove through the superstructure of the *Thunderbolt*. In 1998, the park expanded well beyond its original boundaries with the opening of Lost Kennywood, which recreated the atmosphere of a turn-of-the-century park, complete with *Shoot-the-Chutes*. In 1999, an indoor coaster/dark ride, the *Exterminator*, joined the ride roster while in 2001 Kennywood rebuilt its fearsome *Steel Phantom* coaster into the *Phantom's Revenge*.

Kennywood's successful blending of some of the oldest concepts in amusements with the most modern and up-to-date attractions is truly inspiring. And Kennywood isn't resting on those laurels. As corporations like Six Flags introduce new mega theme parks with mega speed while gobbling up older parks, Kennywood is working on an empire of its own, with nearby Sandcastle waterpark, Idlewild Park at Ligonier, Pennsylvania, and Lake Compounce near Bristol, Connecticut, all having been added to the Kennywood family. Meanwhile, Kennywood's premier entertainment complex continues to live up to its current motto as "America's Finest Traditional Amusement Park."

Lakeside Park, Denver

Lakeside Park is a real trip—right back into the Big Band era. A wonderland of neon and Art Deco awaits patrons passing through the park's entrance tower—a Denver landmark that dates from 1908 when the park opened as White City. Park ownership transferred to a family in 1936, and a daughter from the family, Rhoda Krasner, has been operating the park for many years.

As the name implies, the park sits beside a lake—Lake Rhoda—on Denver's northwest side Berkeley neighborhood along busy Sheridan Road and was only a short walk away from its rival, Elitch Gardens, until that park moved in 1995. In an unconventional twist, Lakeside Park is its own municipality that has its own police force and fire department (but not its own post office). The park occupies an area roughly equal to 32 city blocks.

FOR GOOD TIMES
Lakeside
AMUSEMENT PARK
NORTH SHERIDAN AT I-70 DENVER, COLORADO

28 **BIG THRILL RIDES**
Most exciting variety of rides and amusements in the Rocky Mountain States

14 **KIDDIE RIDES**

VISIT ONE OF AMERICA'S GREAT AMUSEMENT PARKS

Tower entrance at Lakeside Park, Denver, Colorado

The ornate tower of the building that serves as Lakeside Park's entrance and administration building is quite possibly the only surviving example of a Beaux Arts-designed amusement park building from early in the twentieth century. Shown in 1990, the light-bulb-studded structure at one time stood tall above White City amusement park, one of numerous "copycat" parks that sprung up following the success of Coney Island's parks after the turn of the twentieth century.

Lakeside Park and Lake Rhoda

A trip around Lake Rhoda on Lakeside's miniature railroad reveals some breathtaking scenes of the park basking in the setting sun in. The date is 1990, but it could well be a half century earlier.

Cyclone, Lakeside Park, Denver

The boarding station for Lakeside's Big Band-era Cyclone coaster represents Art Deco design and architecture at its best, nicely complementing the Beaux Arts era of the late nineteenth and early twentieth centuries represented by the park's administration building and tower, peeking out above the Cyclone station in the upper background. MIKE SCHAFER

While Elitch Gardens has long been heavily promoted to the general public, Lakeside has instead focused on bookings of large picnic groups from corporations, schools, and churches from all over the Rocky Mountain Front Range region. So, in a sense, the two Denver parks have different audiences.

Amusement park aficionados are quick to laud Lakeside as one of the most beautiful traditional parks that have survived into the new millennium. Indeed, the park's casual atmosphere, coupled to the wondrous array of buildings, rides, trees, and gardens make this a soothing, yet tantalizing, getaway from the all-too-common frenetic atmosphere of theme parks. And what does Lakeside have to offer, in terms of excitement? An intriguing array of rides for adults and tykes alike, the crowning glory of which is the *Cyclone* roller coaster.

Built in 1940 on the site of a huge racing coaster from the White City era, the *Cyclone* is a combined twister/out-and-back ride whose massively Moderne station looks delicious enough to eat. The glowing structure lures unsuspecting first-timers on to a ride that is in reality quite wild and wooly.

One of Lakeside's most historically significant rides rings the lake: the miniature railroad—one of the few amusement park railroads to feature a real, coal-fired steam locomotive (it's from the 1904 St. Louis World's Fair). Many of the other rides and attractions are traditional favorites found at parks everywhere—e.g., *Tilt-A-Whirl*, *Scrambler*, *Spider*—but several have been enhanced by custom neon signage and lighting which must be seen to be believed. In the 1980s, a vicious storm wiped out much of the neon art and other lighting, but Lakeside restored the brilliance soon after.

What a jewel. Don't miss Lakeside.

Playland, Rye, New York

In well-to-do Rye, New York, on the northern shores of Long Island Sound, Paradise Park was a picnic ground gone bad. By the late 1800s, bawdy hotels and rowdy amusement centers were already beginning to crowd the fancier, more exclusive resorts in the area. By the Roaring Twenties, the increasing unsavory flavor of Rye's beach area prompted local residents to demand action of the local government. In the midst of the uproar, Paradise Park burned. To create an amusement area that was more family oriented and respectable—in other words, devoid of prostitutes, drunks, and pickpockets like one might see at nearby Coney Island—the Westchester County

Park Commission purchased Rye Beach and the remains of Paradise Park circa 1927 and leveled them both to create Playland.

Wisely, the Commission turned to outside help to do the job, hiring Frank W. Darling, president of the L. A. Thompson Scenic Railway Company at Coney Island, to construct, operate, and manage Playland. Thompson's splendid Scenic Railways and other coasters and rides could, by this time, be found from coast to coast, so Darling was the perfect choice. He went to work planning the new park. Adhering to the theory that beautiful surroundings attracted beautiful minds, he designed a place *unappealing* to the rowdy and raucous. Construction crews went to work at the close of the 1927 tourist season.

Playland, with its 279 well-groomed acres, originally included picnic areas, restaurants, three ice-skating rinks, a swimming pool, and two beaches totaling approximately 7,900 feet of shoreline, in addition to a stable of thrilling amusement rides.

Playland's design focused on the beauty of architecture in balance. A tree- and flower-bedlined mall flanks the stunning Art Deco Music Tower that can be seen from nearly all parts of the park. Most rides and attractions were fronted by uniform, Art Deco facades. Artists were brought in to produce panels of artwork on the handsome facades, whose main purpose was to defray the sometimes chaotic nature that resulted from simply presenting a series of unrelated rides. Subdued lighting produced a calming effect on park patrons, and an integrated audio system played popular musical

Beach at Playland, Rye, New York

The beach just outside the gates of Playland's amusement area looks much the same as in this 1940s-era postcard. The 279-acre park has been meticulously maintained since it opened in 1928. AUTHOR'S COLLECTION

VIEW FROM THE OCEAN, PLAYLAND, RYE BEACH, N. Y. 34

5A-H2047

Music Tower, Playland

A stunning centerpiece to a stunning amusement park, the Music Tower features a stage for free outdoor concerts. Concessions and rides line either side of this boulevard of flowers and velvety grass. MIKE SCHAFER

Coconut Grove

Santa Cruz Beach Boardwalk, Santa Cruz, California

The only remaining traditional oceanside amusement park on the Pacific coast is but a mountain range away from California's Bay Area. Located on beautiful Monterey Bay, Santa Cruz is an irresistible destination for sun and fun—or perhaps food and drink at one of the many eateries in the Coconut Grove casino.

Flumes and freeways, Santa Cruz

Just what California needs—more freeways! Consider, instead, that Santa Cruz Beach Boardwalk's auto ride is good training for tomorrow's drivers. And environmentalists will love the flume ride: the logs you splash about in are fake. No trees were harmed for this ride! OTTO P. DOBNICK

melodies by Sousa, Wagner, and Berlin over the entire, artfully landscaped grounds.

May 26, 1928, was opening day, and visiting dignitaries immediately proclaimed Playland one of the finest amusement institutions in the country—a claim that holds true today. As with other amusement parks, there was more to Playland than thrill rides and cotton candy. It was a place to see circus acts and concerts, dance under the stars, swim, and win an automobile.

The concept of a family-friendly amusement park appealed to the people of Westchester County and New York City itself. The number of visitors drawn to Playland during its first season far exceeded even the most optimistic predictions. Crowds arrived by auto, bus, trolley, and even by ferries from Long Island and New York City.

Playland's most famous contemporary resident is the *Dragon Coaster*, which is only one year younger than Playland itself. The first coaster at the park was the terrifying *Aeroplane Dips*, which was designed by Fred Church and opened with the park in 1928. To offset the ride's harrowing reputation, the much-gentler *Dragon Coaster* (also of Church design) was added in 1929, and it's been a park favorite ever since. (Insurance problems sealed the fate of the *Aeroplane* in 1957.)

As of 2001, Playland offers nearly 50 rides, including seven classics that pre-date 1930 (the best known, aside from the *Dragon Coaster*, is the *Derby Racer* horse-racing ride, one of only two left in North America; the carousel dates from 1915). Attractions include the House of Mirrors, Haunted Mansion, miniature golf, a beach and a boardwalk, kayaking and boating, ice skating, and picnicking. Playland is unusual these days in that admission to the park is free, just like the old days, and the park offers free concerts as well.

Santa Cruz Beach Boardwalk, Santa Cruz, California

Of the myriad amusement parks that used to dot the West Coast from San Diego to Seattle, only one full-fledged, traditional, oceanside park remains, Santa Cruz Beach Boardwalk, some 60 miles south of San Francisco. This is California's oldest amusement park as well as a State Historical Landmark, with two national historic landmarks—the 1911 Looff carousel and the 1924 *Giant Dipper* roller coaster. Owned and operated by the Santa Cruz Seaside Company since 1915, the Boardwalk remains a family style amusement park, providing guests with a safe, friendly, family experience in the unforgettable atmosphere of a true California beach and the thrills of a classic amusement park.

Santa Cruz Beach Boardwalk boasts its "warm sand, cool surf, and hot rides." Indeed, the beach is a mile long, with plenty of room to soak in that intoxicating California sun. The hottest ride in the adjacent, admission-free amusement area is the second-oldest ride there, the world-class *Giant Dipper*. There's also miniature golf, a flume ride, auto ride, the *Hurricane* metal coaster, Ferris wheel, and—new in 2001—a 3-D fun house and an interactive dark ride called *Ghost Blasters*.

With the loss of such great L.A.-area parks as The Pike at Long Beach and the piers at Venice and Santa Monica, Hollywood had to find another location when it needed an amusement park setting, and Santa Cruz Beach Boardwalk (or, specifically, the *Giant Dipper*) has "starred" in a number of TV commercials, and movies, among them *Sudden Impact*, *The Sting II*, and the vampire classic, *The Lost Boys*.

Life's a beach . . .

. . . and then you fly—on the Sky Ride, that is, over Santa Cruz Beach Boardwalk. At left in this 1987 view, the Giant Dipper looms above the rooftops of the boardwalk's plethora of concession stands and special attractions. OTTO P. DOBNICK

Sleeping Beauty's Castle, Disneyland, Anaheim, California

The symbol of the American theme park may well be this familiar centerpiece to the original Disneyland of 1955 at Anaheim, California, outside Los Angeles. Although Walt Disney was not the inventor of the theme park, he did prove that its concept was viable. WENDELL SAMUELSON

Great Movie Ride, Disney/MGM Studios, Florida

Many modern rides are "virtual reality" rides wherein much of the action is a visual activity that is closely coupled to the ride itself. OTTO P. DOBNICK

VARIATIONS ON A THEME (PARK)
New Twists on Tradition

No matter how you cut it, "fun" is still the name of the game

THEME PARK: n. An amusement park built around a central theme, as a land of fantasy, future world, or past age.

Contrary to popular belief, Walt Disney did not invent the theme park. In fact, what he created was technically not a theme park in the true sense of the word (that is, having a single theme throughout), but rather a new breed of park that presented separate, individually themed areas, grouped together to share some sort of larger theme. Theme parks existed—that is, parks based upon a single overriding theme—long before Disneyland.

What began on Coney Island in New York, like everything else, worked its way west. Sea Lion Park was the first park to charge an entrance admission and use a specific motif—in this case nautical, complete with performing sea lions—to establish a central theme. In the 1940s and 1950s Santa, Mother Goose, and other childhood fairy tales provided the settings and characters—a theme, in other words—at newly established parks, many of them having been built to cater to postwar toddlers.

Today, using a successful economic equation, entertainment companies have taken their movie and television characters and story lines to the parks. Six Flags teamed up with Time Warner to bring *Batman* rides and a Warner Brothers cartoon character decor to parks across the country. Disney produces heroes and heroines, and then complementary lunch boxes, action figures, and finally park rides and costumed characters that give its entertainment mega centers a theme.

Cataloging them is not unlike attempting to keep up with any other retail trend: Beanie Babies, scooters, mood rings or pet rocks.

Santa's Villages and Storylands

A takeoff on some of America's favorite fantasies (at least, those of children), set amusement park attractions in an environment that brings to life people and places children believe exist and

dream of visiting. Recreations of Santa's homestead, complete with elves, workshops, Mrs. Claus, and even reindeer add to the theme. Holiday Land, opening nine years prior to Disneyland as Santa Claus Land in Santa Claus, Indiana, claims to be the first. Many other Santa-themed parks started in the 1940s and 1950s as well, such as Santa's Villages in Skyforest and Scotts Valley, California; Dundee, Illinois; and Jefferson, New Hampshire; along with Santaland USA in Putney, Vermont; and Santa's Workshops in North Pole, New York, and Colorado.

Likewise, the storybook concept plays upon tradition. In Cardiff, New Jersey, Storybook Land has entertained children since the mid 1950s. Aboard the *Storybook Land Express* at Storybook Land in Aberdeen, South Dakota, families cruise the sights of the Land of Oz, including Munchkin Land (*Wizard of Oz* author L. Frank Baum resided in Aberdeen at one point). The Wisconsin Dells is another popular Midwestern destination, with a dizzying array of parks that circle the City of Wisconsin Dells (think of the Dells overall as a land-locked Coney Island). At the Dells, you'll find Storybook Gardens, where children can visit Old MacDonald's Farm and the three little pigs, and ride a 1912 carousel and a miniature train.

Storybook lands are also often found as themed areas of larger parks, like at Idlewild Park near Ligonier, Pennsylvania, providing kiddie rides for children too small or too intimidated to take on major coasters or Ferris wheels. Mother Goose, Sleeping Beauty, and other classic characters are depicted in various art forms—costumed cast members, statues, playground equipment, paintings, and murals—to produce a world straight out of nursery rhymes and fairy tales.

Theme parks based on the Western frontier have been popular since well before the 1950s, like Henry Ford's Greenfield Village in Dearborn, Michigan. Ghost Towns and Frontier Villages, Towns, and Cities once dotted the countryside as Americans took to the road in huge numbers.

Knott's Berry Farm

And then there's the roadside berry stand that became an amusement park. Certainly one of the older theme parks, Knott's Berry Farm also takes its distinction in humble beginnings. In the 1920s the fledgling operation fought with heavy frosts, plummeting berry prices, cash-flow problems and a purchase agreement made during the oil boom of 1927 (which drove land prices sky

Santa's Village, Dundee, Illinois

Santa's Village at Dundee, Illinois, in Chicago's western suburbs, has been entertaining kids since the 1950s. The whole area is themed with a Christmas/North Pole motif. Even traditional rides are given a Christmas look that can be inviting on hot summer days. OTTO P. DOBNICK

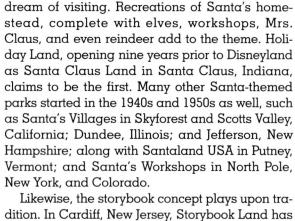

high). Followed soon after by the Great Depression, most people would have been put out of business. However, Walter Knott forged ahead, selling berries from a roadside stand. Their business was doing so well they erected a small berry market, with a tea room where Walter's wife Cordelia served homemade pie and later, her famous chicken dinners. The farm along the highway was called Knott's Berry Place.

As a means of entertaining the restaurant customers standing in line, Walter Knott commissioned an artist to paint a cyclorama of a wagon train crossing the desert in 1940 and eventually brought in actual old buildings to create a more natural atmosphere. They found an old 1868 hotel near Prescott, Arizona, dismantled it and brought it to the farm to house the cyclorama and the Ghost Town was officially underway. Throughout the 1940s, buildings were added—a Kansas schoolhouse and a collection of shacks—mostly from actual "Mother Lode" ghost towns, and in 1947, it became Knott's Berry Farm.

Knott's Berry Farm began its conversion into an amusement park in the 1950s. In 1952 two steam locomotives and a few passenger cars from the Denver & Rio Grande Western Railroad were purchased and transferred to the farm where they were put to work on the Ghost Town & Calico

Railroad. A short time later, a replica of Tombstone Arizona's Birdcage Theater opened in Ghost Town, and productions of daily melodramas were offered.

Disneyland's opening in 1955 brought new business into the area, and Knott's had its biggest year to date. By the end of the decade, the lineup of attractions included the *Haunted Shack*, burro rides, an Indian trading post, Old MacDonald's Farm, a carousel and San Francisco cable cars.

The *Calico Mine Ride* was built by Hurlbut Amusement Company, beginning a longstanding relationship. When it opened in 1960, its use of theming and special effects set a new standard for future Knott's attractions. Now, over 40 years later, the *Calico Mine Ride* anchors the west end of Ghost Town. Arrow Development's log flume, the *Calico Logging Company*, opened in 1969. Designed and constructed by Hurlbut, and later renamed the *Timber Mountain Log Ride*, it was the first heavily themed flume installation.

In 1973, Knott's made history with its first October transformation to "Knott's Scary Farm." The Halloween Haunt is reputed to be the first Halloween event in an amusement park—an event that is now an annual tradition at parks across the land. A few years later Knott's would elaborate on

Sea World, San Antonio, Texas

The beautiful Steel Eel swoops above the heads of patrons at Sea World in San Antonio in 1999. At the park's lake, aquatic shows run throughout the day. Is this an amusement park, animal park, or theme park? Yes.

the holiday conversion and offer "Knott's Merry Farm" to winter visitors.

Knott's added Fiesta Village and Roaring 20's with the latter being the largest expansion and expenditure in the park's history to date. Major attractions included the *Corkscrew* roller coaster (the first such coaster), *Motorcycle Chase*, the *Sky Tower/Sky Jump* and *Knott's Bear-y Tales*. By the late 1970s, *Montezooma's Revenge*, an Intamin/Schwartzkopf shuttle-loop roller coaster, had opened in Fiesta Village.

Cordelia Knott died in 1974. Flags in Buena Park flew at half-mast when Walter passed on in 1981, and in 1983 professional, outside management was brought in for the first time. The Roaring '20s was re-themed into the Boardwalk and welcomed a new racing looping steel roller coaster, the *Windjammer*, in 1997, the same year that Knott's Berry Farm became part of the Cedar Fair, Ltd. (of Cedar Point fame) family of fun parks that runs many of the survivors. The following year, *Ghost Rider*, a wooden roller coaster, opened to rave reviews.

Animal Parks

The aquatic concept of Coney's Sea Lion Park was reintroduced when Marineland of the Pacific was built in 1954 on the Palos Verdes peninsula in Southern California. An offshoot of Marine Studios in Florida, Marineland paved the way for the subsequent Sea World parks. Marineland is gone, but Sea World became a survivor as part of the Busch Gardens family of parks. Having grown from the original in San Diego to include parks in Orlando and San Antonio, Sea World is now seeing a shift to thrill rides.

Busch Gardens itself started with an animal theme, opening in 1959 as a bird sanctuary, on a 16-acre tract next to Busch's Tampa brewery. Begun as a public relations project, it was expanded in the 1960s to a zoological park with an African veldt theme. Finally in 1971 the park was expanded to include multiple themed areas, and the name was expanded to Busch Gardens–The Dark Continent, a reference to its African theme. Now, with a much greater emphasis on thrill rides, the park is known simply as Busch Gardens Tampa Bay.

Busch Entertainment Corporation has gone on to be one of the largest adventure park operators in America. Busch Gardens Williamsburg (originally The Old Country) has operated on 360 acres of lush Virginia countryside adjacent to the James River since 1975. Awarded the honor of being one of the most beautiful theme parks in the U.S., the park provides an enchanted adventure through European legends with a wide variety of thrills and all-family rides, shows and exhibits.

Lion Country Safari and Marine World Africa U.S.A. made big splashes in the 1970s, but found it hard to sustain themselves as animal-only attractions. While Lion Country closed most of its parks, Marine World moved from burgeoning Redwood City, California, across the bay to Vallejo, added rides, and now calls itself Six Flags Marine World.

Disneyland

When Disneyland opened on July 17, 1955, the face of the American amusement park was forever changed. Whatever Walter Elias Disney may or may not have invented, there can be no doubt that he had a dramatic effect on the character of the amusement facility as we know it today. The folks who developed Disneyland—as well as subsequent Disney parks and World's Fair attractions—became known as "Imagineers," a moniker Walt invented. Although reflective of its roots, Disneyland was not the movies. It was a product and reflection of the medium that, after World War II, brought the traditional amusement park to its knees: television. A Disneyland "guest"—as patrons became known—could stand at the hub at the end of Main Street and decide whether to visit Adventureland, Frontierland, Fantasyland, or Tomorrowland, as though they were operating some cosmic remote control.

When Walt Disney's daughters were young, he took them to an amusement park to ride the

merry-go-round. Eventually he conjured up the idea of a family park for parents and their children to enjoy together. When he moved his studio from Hyperion Avenue to its present location in Burbank, his earliest imaginings were of a magical little park adjacent to the new studio, about eight acres in size, with such things as singing waterfalls and statues of the famous Disney characters. It would be a place where visitors could actually meet Mickey and pose for pictures.

For years, Disney had been getting requests for studio tours, and letters from children wanting to see where Mickey Mouse lived. Shortly after the move to the new studio, the first Disney film to feature extensive live action footage was released. The year was 1941: "The Reluctant

Dragon" featured footage of the new studio and public interest in visiting Mickey's home escalated.

Upon America's involvement in World War II, Disney's animated characters were enlisted to star in training and morale films for the war effort. But by the end of the war, Disney's thoughts had returned to his dream of an alternative to those grubby little parks he had frequented with his girls. The catalyst came when he and animator Ward Kimball set off from Pasadena aboard Santa Fe's *Super Chief* for a visit to the 1948–49 Chicago Railroad Fair. While that exposition had a dramatic effect on Walt, their stop at Henry Ford's Greenfield Village, a park designed to showcase the great inventors, really got Disney's wheels turning. He saw

A Mickey Mouse operation . . .

. . . and proud of it. In an aerial photo dating from circa 1966, the park that changed the face of the American amusement park is shown in all its sprawling glory at Anaheim, California. Walt Disney may not have invented the theme park (or themed park), but he showed everyone how to do it right. At left foreground is Frontierland while at right, largely hidden in the trees, is Adventureland. Main Street USA is just above, and Tomorrowland is at upper right center. The Matterhorn Bobsled stands prominent among all the park's attractions.
AUTHOR'S COLLECTION

Main Street USA, Disneyland

The heart of Disneyland (as well as the Magic Kingdom at Walt Disney World in Florida) is Main Street USA, a slightly under-scale replica of an American city in the late 1800s. Crowds are free to wander the sidewalks as well as the streets (there are no autos to dodge, just the after effects of the occasional horse-drawn streetcar). This view of the Anaheim park's principal artery is shown in 1965. WENDELL SAMUELSON

reminders of his childhood—a town square, a main street, a railroad station—that would later emerge as his opening theme on the land across from the studio. It was about sixteen acres, a suitable size for his Mickey Mouse Park. On March 27, 1952, the *Burbank Daily Review* broke the story of Disney's plans to build a $1.5 Million dream park called Disneyland. But the city council was not about to sanction a kiddieland, carney atmosphere or squawking merry-go-round in the city of Burbank. The result is almost 74 acres of Disneyland in Anaheim instead. Many Disney rides have become household names like, *Space Mountain*, the famous *Matterhorn*, the *Pirates of the Caribbean*, and the *Haunted Mansion*—dubbed the best dark ride ever.

Walt Disney World

Opening in Lake Buena Vista, Florida, in 1971, Walt Disney World is roughly four times the size of Manhattan, has four theme parks, three waterparks, a stadium, an auto-racing complex, campground, countless hotels, and shopping areas—it is a virtual amusement complex.

The quintessential Disney park, the Magic Kingdom is the spacious, full-scale counterpart to Disneyland. Its themed areas—Main Street USA, Frontierland, Adventureland, and Tomorrowland among them—transport visitors to a place where the cares of the outside world seem to magically

melt away. Like Disneyland, the park is built on a wheel/spoke design with the Cinderella Castle in the center of the wheel and the different themed lands emanating from the center.

Epcot, originally known as EPCOT Center, is more a collection of interactive exhibits than a theme park. Originally envisioned by Walt Disney as an Experimental Prototype Community Of Tomorrow, it was designed to incorporate the best ideas of industry, government, and academia worldwide. Opened in 1982, Epcot has two themes: a showcase of American industry and research, schools, and cultural and educational opportunities; and a tour of the countries of the world, fashioned as a sort of permanent world's fair.

The 1989 addition, Disney/MGM Studios Theme Park—the third theme park to open at Walt Disney World—is a tribute to the classic films of Hollywood and the magic of Disney movie-making. In addition to rides and shows, this park gives a glimpse into a real (if small) working movie and television studio, as well as one of Disney's animation production units.

The feel is Hollywood in the golden age of the 1940s, when Walt Disney created some of his greatest feature-length animated films. The park's architecture recalls elements of Art Deco mixed with California crazy styles, along with a few

uniquely Disney touches, like the Earful Tower—a water tower complete with mouse ears.

The movie ride in the Chinese Theater is a real MGM attraction. Real props and costumes from Hollywood classics are displayed in the queue area and old-style movie previews are played on a giant screen in a room designed to look like Hollywoodland (the old hilltop sign is there, too). Moving theater cars take riders off on a movie-making adventure. Scenes from old silent films give way to classics such as *Mary Poppins*, *Casablanca*, the original *Tarzan the Ape Man*, and *Alien*.

Known as Disney's "new species of theme park," the 1998 Animal Kingdom has a relaxed atmosphere, elaborate theming and a lush tropical feel. The attractions naturally come from the more outdoorsy flicks like *Pocahontas*, *A Bug's Life*, and *The Lion King*.

Since heat and humidity are part of Florida life year around, it is a natural site for a waterpark. From the earliest days of Walt Disney World, imagineers have worked water into the scheme. When River Country's imaginative waterpark opened, it was one of the first of its kind in the country. With the addition of Typhoon Lagoon and Blizzard Beach, the ordinary became extraordinary: now there is always "snow" in Florida.

Six Flags Over Everywhere

The first successful theme park to follow Disneyland's 1955 smash hit, Six Flags Over Texas opened in 1961, waving its flag motif and offering rides in six themed areas: Spain, France, Mexico, the Confederacy, the United States, and the Republic of Texas. A project of Randall Duell & Associates, the park had a good location (at Arlington, Texas, between Dallas and Fort Worth) and good financial backing.

Unlike its two unsuccessful predecessors built by Duell—Pleasure Island in Massachusetts and Freedomland in the Bronx, New York—Six Flags embraced thrill rides. Among the unique rides are the *Texas Chute Out*, a 200-foot-tall parachute ride; *Speelunker's Cave*, a dark ride through winding waterways; and actual antique steam trains that once hauled Louisiana sugar cane. Wood coasters arrived with the *Judge Roy Scream* in 1982, and in 1990, the *Texas Giant* came to town. The largest of its kind at the time, the wooden behemoth quickly rose to the Number One position on many coaster enthusiasts top-ten lists and in many cases retains that position today. The newest coaster, *Titan*, is a steel superstructure towering 255 feet above the earth. It features an amazing drop at a thrilling 85 MPH and over a mile of twisting spirals.

Disney/MGM Studios Theme Park

A panoramic camera scoops in the astonishing array of visuals that line the streets of the new Disney/MGM Studios Theme Park at Walt Disney World near Orlando, Florida. There are shows galore, but there are thrill rides as well. The slightly ominous Hollywood Hotel looming in the distance is in part a walk-through attraction as well as a free-fall gravity ride.

Six Flags Over Georgia, originally opened in 1967 in Mableton, just outside of Atlanta. Themed areas cover 276 acres and offer the classic PTC five-abreast carousel imported from Chicago's late lamented Riverview Park. In 1973, the *Great American Scream Machine*, a 105-foot tall wooden roller coaster, began the mega-coaster competition among parks, for the world's tallest/ longest/fastest roller coaster.

The newest rides hold to the park's reputation for innovative thrills. *Acrophobia* (the term for an unnatural dread of heights) is a 200-foot rotating tower drop ride. Six Flags Over Georgia's super boomerang roller coaster, *Deja Vu*, was the world's tallest and fastest of its kind when it opened, with a brand new twist for boomerang-type (forward and backward) coasters—riders are carried in ski-lift-style chairs suspended from the track above.

In 1971 the third in Six Flags' family opened: Six Flags Over Mid-America near St. Louis. It includes a unique area themed to Missouri history with exhibits from the 1904 St. Louis World Fair. The park features the *Screamin' Eagle*, a classic John Allen wood coaster that was added in 1976 and at the time was billed as the longest, tallest and fastest coaster in the world. While the park has done a good job of keeping pace with the business of thrill rides, it has learned that roller coasters are what's really bringing in the crowds. As of the 2001 season, a massive world-class wooden roller coaster graces the skyline of what is now called Six Flags St. Louis. *The Boss* has an unprecedented double down double-drop first hill of 150 feet, two additional drops of no less than 103 feet, numerous high-banked turns, and a 570 degree helix.

Moving into the new millennium, Six Flags, Inc. (Formerly Premier Parks, Inc.) and its subsidiaries own or operate 35 parks—including 27 domestic parks, one in Mexico, and seven in Europe. Six Flags theme parks generally offer a broad selection of state-of-the-art and traditional thrill rides and water attractions, along with themed areas, concerts, shows, restaurants, and game venues. Among the existing traditional parks that the company has taken over are Riverside Park near Springfield, Massachusetts, and Geauga Lake near Cleveland, Ohio. The later acquisition also

Six Flags guidebook, 1960s

Six Flags Over Texas published this elaborate, four-color guidebook to sell at the park as a souvenir. This was the first Six Flags park. AUTHOR'S COLLECTION

Six Flags St. Louis

Six Flags makes sure that each of its parks feature the latest in thrill innovations. Mr. Freeze is a shuttle-type coaster that takes riders up a 90-degree incline—then down, backward. Wood coasters await the less radically inclined.

included adjacent Sea World, thus Six Flags has announced plans to create a new mega-park out of the two. Six Flags Worlds of Adventure will feature three extraordinary parks in one—a thrill ride park, a marine park, and a water park.

Paramount Parks

A division of Viacom Inc., Paramount Parks is one of the largest theme-park companies in the world and entertains approximately 13 million visitors annually at its five North American parks and interactive attraction Star Trek: The Experience at the Las Vegas Hilton. Paramount's claim, that "the thrills are Paramount" certainly applies to the connection between its amusement park attractions and the other entertainment they produce.

The Paramount line-up includes sister parks Kings Island near Cincinnati, Ohio, and Kings Dominion, in Doswell, just north of Richmond, Virginia. Carowinds straddles the North Carolina-South Carolina state line. Originally the project of a local developer, it was later sold to Family Leisure Centers, Inc., who owned the Kings parks. Paramount's (formerly Marriott's) Great America, in Santa Clara is one of Northern California's most thrilling parks, in operation since 1976.

Universal Studios

In the late 1960s and early 1970s, Universal Studios, just north of Hollywood, began offering tours, giving visitors a glimpse of what television and movie production was like. The tram tours are still a centerpiece, although a host of thrill rides and attractions have been added over the years, as well as live shows. The Universal Studios Theme Park claims to have more Hollywood entertainment to offer than any other destination in the world. The attractions come right out of the movies and favorite television shows. *The Terminator 2:3D*, a time-travel attraction, puts visitors in the middle of a cyber war, with explosions and laser fire galore. *Jurassic Park–The Ride* brings the prehistoric era to life in an incredible jungle water ride that includes spitters, raptors, and the towering and fearsome Tyrannosaurus Rex.

Kings Island, Kings Mill, Ohio

Paramount's Kings Island is arguably the Midwest's best theme park, thanks to beautiful landscaping, heavy promotion, and top-notch rides and attractions. The looping coaster in this 1987 view from the park's replica Eiffel Tower is the King Cobra, first to introduce stand-up coastering to America. MIKE SCHAFER

In May 1999, Universal Studios got into the amusement industry in a 110-acre way, offering Walt Disney World some daunting competition with its new Islands of Adventure theme park. "Why just watch the movies when you can live them?" they invite tourists to consider. Opening in Orlando, Florida, with 23 rides, the park features five themed areas: Marvel Super Hero Island, Toon Lagoon, Jurassic Park, Lost Continent, and Seuss Landing. It has three high-speed roller coasters (the *Incredible Hulk* and inverted twin *Dueling Dragons*) plus *The Amazing Adventures of Spiderman*, a one-of-a-kind simulator that combines 3-D and live motion. Milder theme rides and play zone attractions are available to meet the needs of families with small and/or less daring children.

Post Theme-Era Parks

Since the early 1960s, the trend in amusement park development has been toward the large regional theme parks. However, in the late 1980s, a new concept began to emerge that would bring the amusement park back to the local level—the family fun park. These parks had their start as a result of the miniature golf renaissance in the 1960s. Most of the courses born in the 1960s were swallowed up by suburban development, but of those that remained, many began to grow with the addition of other attractions like batting cages, go-karts, bumper cars, bumper boats and water slides.

Huish Family Fun Centers began in the late 1950s with an 18-hole mini-golf course on a former junkyard site in La Mesa California. They added parks and attractions like trampolines, go-karts, bumper boats, and batting cages, but always worked around miniature golf as the central theme. When the La Mesa park was sold for freeway expansion, the Huish family opened a center in Vista. There are also Huish Family Fun Centers in El Cajon, Fountain Valley, and Anaheim, California.

The antithesis, in a sense, of the gargantuan theme parks and their never-ending lines and wandering oversized, cartoon characters, Golf 'N Stuff parks (in Norwalk and Ventura, California, and Tucson, Arizona) feature fountains, topiary sculptures, and themed landscapes like a Spanish Mission motif or an Arabian Knight castle. Typical mini-golf elements—windmills, castles, lighthouses, clocktowers—combine with some unusual elements. Gazebos and other shade-producing structures are strategically placed around the golf courses, while well-integrated rides (bumper boats, *Lit'l Indy* tracks, and *Ram Rods*) provide visual stimulation as well as something else to do. At the Tucson park, waterfalls and waterways are in abundance, running to and from a central pool, plus honest-to-goodness grass, a real novelty in sun-baked Arizona.

Castles & Coasters, Phoenix, Arizona

Proving that coasters remain a huge drawing card for amusement areas, specialty parks that cater to fans of miniature golf, go-carts, and the like have been adding coasters to their "portfolios" of late. Castles & Coasters at Phoenix is ostensibly first and foremost a miniature golf park, but as this 1995 photo reveals, coasters and flume rides have become par for the course(s).

Amusement Park Deja Vu

Although without intending to, Walt Disney exerted an incredible influence over amusement park history when he created Disneyland, the home of Mickey Mouse. His vision was of a place people could visit that would satiate their curiosity about the television and movie studios. Now,

several parks, one Disney among them, are built upon that very theme: operational or model television and movie studios.

Another irony: Disney's newest park, California Adventure, which is adjacent to Disneyland and opened in February of 2001, has among its themed sections Paradise Pier, an area replicating the beloved old traditional boardwalk parks, including a white-structured roller coaster (although it looks like an old-fashioned wooden ride, it's all steel). In fact, the carousel carries ornamental plaques commemorating Playland Park at San Francisco; Looff Pier, Lick Pier, and others on Santa Monica Bay; The Pike at Long Beach; and parks at other California locations! Somehow the cornerstone of amusement park history came full circle and is a part of the amusement park future as well.

Paradise Pier carousel, Anaheim, California

Look closely at the decorative plaques on the carousel in the Paradise Pier section of Disney's new California Adventure theme park, and you'll see references to California amusements parks of the past. The amusement park has come full circle (pun intended)!

Paradise Pier: old is new

Coney Island as well as West Coast parks are alive and well at Paradise Pier, one of the themed areas within Disney's new California Adventure theme park adjacent to good old Disneyland. The pleasure wheel is a direct takeoff on Wonder Wheel at Coney Island, while the whole area simulates a pier-type park once so common on the California coast. Although it looks like a traditional wood coaster, the Paradise Pier ride is an all-steel looper—the loop itself encircles the Micky Mouse profile on the side of the coaster—that operates in part by linear induction.

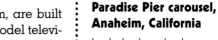

INDEX

Aerial Night Attacks, 30
Aerio Cycle, 28
Aeroplane coaster, 53, 58, 104, 142
Aladdin's Castle, 67
Alcoke, Charles, 98
Allen, John, 104, 106, 107, 132, 152
Americana Park, 101
American Merry-Go-Round & Novelty Company, 81
Animal Kingdom, 151
Aquarasel, 123
Arrow Development/Dynamics, 90, 103, 105, 109, 110, 147
Astroland, 33, 35
AstroWorld, 108, 109
Autopia, 91

Backety-Back Scenic, 116
Bacon, Alexander, 22
Bat, The, 109
Batman–The Ride, 105, 110, 146
Beacon Tower, 31
Beast, 108
Beecher, Lina, 38
Belmont Park, 43, 102
Bessemer & Lake Erie Railroad, 51
Big Bad Wolf, 109
Big Dipper (Calif.), 46, 48
Big Dipper (Ohio), 102
Big Eli Ferris wheel, 84, 86
Big Scenic, 121
Birdcage Theater, 147
Bluebeard's Palace, 114, 129
Blue Streak, 105, 131, 132
Bobs coasters at . . .
    California, 47, 48
    Illinois 107, 124
    New York (Coney), 32
    Wisconsin, 55
Bollinger & Mabillard, 105
Boss, The, 152
Bostock's Circus, 31
Boston, Revere Beach & Lynn Railroad, 14
Boyton, Paul, 13, 23, 25, 88
Brandywine Express, 102
Bright, Oliver, 40–41
Brighton Beach, 20
Buckroe Beach, 42, 56
Bungarz Team Wagon & Carrousele Works, 81
Burnham, Daniel H., 12, 14, 44
Busch Gardens Tampa Bay, 105, 110, 111, 148
Busch Gardens Williamsburg, 75, 109, 148

Camden Park, 126
Cages of Wild Wolves, 25
Calico Mine Ride, 147
California Adventure, 154–155
Canals of Venice, 89–90
Carolwood Pacific, 95
Carowinds, 110, 153
Cascade Park, 50
Cascades, 114
Castles & Coasters, 59, 154
Cat Pitch, 62
Cedar Point, 82, 90, 105, 109, 110, 128–130
Celeron Park, 114
Centennial Exposition, 1876, 12, 22, 95
Century Flyer coaster car, 105
Chang, 110
Chance Manufacturing Company/Rides Inc., 86, 95

Chicago Railroad Fair, 149
Chinese Theater ride, 151
Church, Fred, 36, 102, 104–105, 129, 142
Circle Swing, 83
Cobb, William, 104-105
Columbia Gardens, 17
Comet Flyer, 52
Comet (Pa.), 103
Comet (Canada), 116, 117
Coney Island (N.Y.), 12, 13, 14, 17, 18-35, 36, 37, 38, 39, 43, 48, 58, 59, 71–74, 84, 88, 91, 94, 98, 99, 100, 101, 104, 107, 108, 113, 132, 138, 140, 146, 155
Coney Island (Ohio), 17, 53, 114–116
Conneaut Lake Park, 51, 71, 76, 105, 130-132
Corkscrew, 107, 147
Cornball Express, 111
Crown Metal Products, 95
Crystal Beach, 60, 92, 104, 116–118
Custom Coasters International (CCI), 105, 111
Cyclone coasters at . . .
    Colorado, 96, 104
    New York, 18, 32, 33, 34, 35, 104, 108
    New Jersey, 121
    Ohio, 128, 129
    Ontario, 104, 117
Cyclone Racer, 107, 123

Dante's Inferno, 92
Darkness and Dawn, 27–28
Davidson, George, 51
Deja Vu, 105
Deno's Wonder Wheel Park, 33, 35
Dentzel family, 79-80
Dentzel Co., 132, 136, 137
Denver & Rio Grande Western Railroad, 147
Derby (Calif.), 46
Derby/Derby Racer (Ohio), 106, 119
Devil's Gorge, 55
Devil's Kitchen, 114
Dinn, Charlie, 105
Dinn-Larrick, Denise, 105
Dip the Dips, 104
Disney, Walter Elias, 11, 12, 14, 92, 103, 148
Disneyland, 54, 90, 91, 103, 147, 148–150
Disney/MGM Studios Theme Park, 150
Dorney Park, 78, 83, 132–133
Down & Out Slide, 30
Dragon Coaster, 58, 142
Dragon Gorge Scenic Railway, 45, 46
Dragon Slide, 49
Dreamland (Coney Island), 21, 31–32, 36, 37, 58, 59, 88, 113
Dreamland (Rochester), 54
Drop the Dip (N.Y.), 101
Drop the Dips, 30,
Dundy, Elmer "Skip", 28, 29, 88

Eiffel Tower, 12
Electric Park, 54, 88
Eli Bridge Company, 86
Elitch Gardens, 8, 61, 85, 104, 106, 133-134
Epicycloidal Diversion, 84
Epcot Center, 150
Euclid Beach, 53, 83, 106, 118–119
Eye-Full Tower, 124
Eyerly Aircraft, 86

Feltman Carousel, 81
Feltman, Charles, 71–72
Ferris Jr., George, 12, 84
Feucht, Christopher, 101
Figure-8 coaster, 99
Fire and Flames, 29
Fireball, 107
Flash, 107, 123
Flip-Flap, (N.J.) 38
Flip-Flap (N.Y.), 25
Flying Circus, 44, 48, 49, 84
Flying Turns coasters in . . .
    Ohio, 106–107
    Illinois, 124
    New Jersey, 122
Forrester, Issac N., 84
Fraser, Alexander, 46

Gallup's Grove, 17
Geauga Lake, 102, 152
Gee Whiz, 124
Giant Coaster, 116, 117
Giant Cyclone Safety Coasters, 104, 116
Giant Dipper coasters at . . .
    Santa Monica, 44
    San Diego, 102
    Santa Cruz, 143
    Venice, 47, 48, 49
Giant SeeSaw, 28
Gillie, Godard & Company, 81
Giradela Tower, 31, 32
Golf 'N' Stuff, 154
Go-Karts, 91
Grand Canyon Electric Railroad, 46
Great America, 53, 153
Great American Revolution, 105, 108
Great Coasters International, (GCI) 105, 111
Great Escape, 117
Great Nor'easter, 104
Great White, 40, 104
Greenfield Village, 146, 149
Greyhound, 105
Gumpertz, Sam, 31, 58, 59
Gwazi, 105, 111

Handwerker, Nathan, 73–74
Haunted Castle, 68, 92
Haunted Mansion, 93, 150
Haunted Swing, 32
Hell Gate, 32
Herschell, Allen, 80, 81, 82
Herschell Co., 81
Hershey Park, 102–103, 111
High Boy, 50
Hi-Striker, 63
Holiday World, 111
Huish Family Fun Centers, 154
Human Roulette Wheel, 67
Humphrey III, Dudley S., 118
Hurlbut Amusements, 147, 148
Hurricane, 143

Idlewild, 5, 138, 146
Idora Park, 112, 119-121
Indiana beach, 67
Infant Incubator, 32, 46,
Ingersoll, Frederick, 37, 54, 104, 128, 136
Intamin/Schwartzkopf, 105, 148
Invertigo, 105
Islands of Adventure, 154

Jack Rabbit, 104, 120
Jones Woods, 17, 79
Journey to the Center of the Earth, 132
Jurassic Park–The Ride, 153

Kenny, Anthony, 51

Kenny's Grove, 51
Kennywood, 16, 51, 52, 53, 58, 61, 65, 7, 81, 84, 89, 104, 130, 135–138
Kentucky Kingdom, 110
Kiddieland, 79, 95
King Cobra, 109
Kings Dominion, 110, 153
Kings Island, 105, 107, 108, 109, 111, 114, 153
Kinney, Abbott, 43, 44
Kinney Pier, 44, 45
Kinney, Thorton, 46
Knoebels Grove/Amusement Resort, 23, 72, 92
Knott Family, 23
Knott's Berry Farm, 90, 107, 128, 146–148,

Lackawanna & Wyoming Valley Railway, 52
Lagoon Park, 16, 90, 95
Lake Compounce, 17, 104, 138
Lakeside Park, 56, 66, 85, 88, 95, 96, 126, 139–140
Lakewood Park, 112
La Monica Pier, 36–37
Leap Frog Scenic Railway, 129
Lenape Park, 102
Lightening Racer, 49
Lilliputia, 31
Loop the Loop
    New Jersey, 38
    New York, 23, 25,
Los Angeles Pacific Railway, 43, 44
Lost Kennywood, 138
Lost River, 92, 121
Luna III, 29
Luna Parks in . . .
    Ohio, 53, 54
    New York, 18, 26, 27, 28–31, 35, 36, 37, 82, 84, 88, 91, 133
    Pennsylvania, 36, 54

Magnum XL-200, 105, 110, 130
Mangels, William, 84
Manhattan Beach, 20
Mantis, 130
Mariner's Landing, 39
Matterhorn Bobsleds, 103, 149, 150
Mauch Chunk-Summit Hill & Switch Back Railway, 98
McKane, John Y., 21–23, 72
Mellon, Andrew, 51
Merry Mix Up, 82
Michigan's Adventure, 105, 108
Midway Park, 113–114
Mile Sky Chaser, 30
Millenium Force, 10, 1309
Miller, John, 101, 106, 114, 121, 137
Million Dollar Coaster, 53
Million Dollar Pier, 39, 46
Milwaukee Electric Railway & Light Company, The, 53
Minature Train Company, 94, 95
Mindbender, 105
Miracle Strip, 42
Mister Twister, 85, 104, 106, 134
Monongahela Street Railway, 51, 52
Montu, 110
Morey's Pier, 39, 104
Mountain Park, 71
Mr. Freeze, 152
Mr. Toad's Wild Ride, 92
Mullers, Albert and Daniel, 81
Municipal Pier, 36–37
Myrtle Beach, 42

Mystery Island Banana Train, 50
Mystery Shack, 67
Mystic Maze, 46

Nathan's, 32
National Amusement Devices (NAD), 105, 122, 131, 137
Nickel Empire, 21, 32-34
Noah's Ark (Calif.), 48
Noah's Ark (Pa.), 137

Ocean Park, 43, 45, 48, 49, 50
Ocean View Park, 42
Ohio Grove, 53, 114
Old Mill, 89, 90
Old Orchard Beach, 43
Olmsted, Frederick L., 12, 14
Outer Limits: Flight of Fear, 111
Over The Falls (N.Y.), 90
Over The Falls (Calif.), 48

Pacific Electric Railway, 44
Pacific Ocean Park, 48, 50, 113
Pacific Park, 43
Pair-O-Chutes, 124
Palisades Park, 84, 113, 121–123
Paradise Park, 140
Paradise Pier, 155
Paramount, 111, 153
Park & Falls Street Railway, 119
Pavilion of Fun, 65
Phantom's Revenge, 138
Philadelphia Toboggan Company (PTC), 10, 11, 46, 52, 63, 81, 82, 90, 102, 103, 104–105, 107, 117, 123, 124, 125, 134, 152
Phoenix Iron Works, 84
Pickering Pleasure Pier, 46
Pike, The, 50, 107, 113, 122, 123, 142, 155
Pippin, 123, 137
Pirates of the Caribbean, 92, 93, 150
Pitney, Dr. Jonathan, 39
Pittsburgh Railways, 52
Playland-at-the-Beach, 50, 155
Playland Park, 58, 82, 140–142
Ponce de Leon Park, 16
Prior & Church, 36, 81, 102, 104–105, 124
Prior, Thomas, 36, 102, 104–105
Pullman-Standard, 95
Puzzletown, 125

Race Thru The Clouds, 46, 94, 104
Racer, 107, 128
Racing Coaster, 55, 106
Racing Derby, 81, 106
Rampage, 86
Raptor, 111
Rattlesnake Rapids, 90
Raven, 111
Revere Beach, 42, 66
Riverside Grove, 17
Riverside Park, 15, 152
Riverview, 53, 55, 58, 67, 81, 84, 88, 106, 113, 123–125
Roar, 105, 111
Robinson Park, 86
Rock-O-Plane, 85
Rocky Glen Park, 52, 53
Rocky Point Park, 87
Rosenthal, Jack and Irving, 121
Russian Mountains, 10, 97
Ryan, Francis, 43, 44

Safety coasters, 102
St. Louis World's Fair (1904), 74, 95, 128, 140, 152

Saltair, 51, 52
Salt Lake, Garfield & Western Railroad, 52
Santa Cruz Beach Boardwalk, 50, 80, 142, 143
Santa Fe Railway, 43, 149
Santa's Villages, 146
Satellite, 85
Sawyer Observatory, 12, 22
Scenic-type railways, 13, 39, 99, 119, 128, 136
Scenic Railway (Venice), 99
Scenic Railway (Ohio), 130
Schmeck, Herbert, 102, 104
Schofield, George W., 89
Scrambler, 140
Screamin' Eagle, 152
Scream Machine, 96
Screechin' Eagle, 101
Seabreeze Park, 76, 81, 90
Sea Lion Park, 20, 23, 25, 26, 88, 146, 148
Seaplane, 136
Sea Serpent, 50
Sea World, 108, 148
Serpentine Railway, 99
Shivering Timbers, 105
Shockwave, 105
Shoot-the-Chutes
    California, 48
    Colorado, 88
    Illinois, 54, 123
    New York, 23, 29, 30
    Pennsylvania, 53, 138
Side-friction coaster, 99-101
Six Flags parks in . . .
    California, 105, 107, 110, 111, 148
    Georgia, 81, 104, 105, 152
    Illinois, 82, 105, 110
    Maryland, 105
    Massachusetts, 15, 17
    Missouri, 104, 152
    New Jersey, 110
    Ohio, 102, 104, 131, 152
    Texas, 90, 95, 103, 151
Skee Ball, 63, 65, 115
Skydiver, 86, 87
Sky Rocket, 114, 121
Sky Wheel, 86
Soak City, 130
Some Kick, 47
Son of Beast, 111
Southern Pacific Railroad, 95
Spider, 140
Spillman Engineering, 81
Splash Mountain, 90
Splashwater Falls, 89
Space Mountain, 150
Splash Mountain, 90
Splashwater Falls, 89
Stauch, Louis, 73
Steam Riding Gallery, 80
Steel Force, 133
Steel Pier, 39
Steeplechase, 25
Steeplechase Island, 54
Steeplechase Park, 13, 21, 24, 25–28, 34, 35, 54, 65
Steeplechase Pier, 38, 39, 54
Stein & Goldstein, 81
Storylands, 146
Sullivan, William E., 84
Summit Beach Park, 12, 53
Switchback Railway, 98–99, 119
Swooper, 86

Taft Broadcasting, 114–115
Terminator 2:3D, 153
Texas Chute Out, 151
Texas Cyclone, 104
Thompson, Frederic, 28–29, 88
Thompson, La Marcus, 39, 45, 98, 99, 118, 128, 141
Thriller, 106, 107, 118, 119

Thru the Falls, 30
Thunderbolt coasters at . . .
    Connecticut, 43
    New York, 32
    Pennsylvania, 84, 138
Tickler, 84
Tidal Wave, 89
Tig'rr, 111
Tilt-A-Whirl, 76, 85, 140
Tilyou, George, 13, 24, 25-26, 28 50, 65
Timber Mountain Log Ride, 90
Tipsy House, 67
Titan, 151
Tivoli Gardens, 8, 11
Toboggan Slide, 10, 15
Tom Thumb Golf, 68–70
Top Gun, 110
Traver Engineering Co., 82, 104, 116, 119, 121, 136
Traver, Harry G., 82, 104–105, 12, 136
Trip to the Moon, 27
Trocadero Ballroom, 134
Tsunami, 89,
Tumble Bug,132, 137
Tumbler, 86
Tunnel of Love, 90
Turbo, 86
Turkey Trot, 30
Turtle Chase, 82
Twenty Thousand Leagues Under the Sea, 29

Universal Studios, 92, 153

Vasona Park, 94
Vauxhall Gardens, 10, 16, 79
Vekoma, 105
Velvet Coaster, 123
Venice Pier, 45, 84, 94
Venice Scenic Railroad, 45, 46
Vettel family 105, 128
Virginia Reel, 122
Vortex, 105, 109

Walt Disney World, 12, 14, 93, 150-151
West Brighton, 20
Whalom Park, 15, 52, 86
Whip, 84
Whirlwind Giant Dipper, 104
White City (World's Columbian Exposition), 13, 14
White City (Ill.), 54, 55, 74
White City (Colo.), 88
Whitney, George, 50
Wildcat coasters at . . .
    Connecticut, 104
    Pennsylvania, 111
    Ohio (Youngstown), 112–113, 120, 121
    Ohio (Cincinnati), 114
Wild Mouse, 137
Wild Wheels Pier, 39, 40
Wild Wheels Raceway and Adventure Park, 40
Wildwood, 39-42, 104
Willow Grove Park, 52, 100
Witching Waves, 91
Wonderland, 13
Wonder Wheel, 32, 33, 35, 155
World Exposition (Paris, 1889), 12
World's Columbian Exhibition (Chicago, 1893), 10, 12, 13, 25, 44, 54, 55, 58, 73, 84
Wormwood's Monkey Theater, 29

XLR8, 109

Zipper, 86
Zombie, 92